AMERICAN IMPERIALISM IN 1898

Problems in American Civilization

UNDER THE EDITORIAL DIRECTION OF

George Rogers Taylor

AMERICAN IMPERIALISM IN 1898

EDITED WITH AN INTRODUCTION BY
Theodore P. Greene

Problems in American Civilization

READINGS SELECTED BY THE
DEPARTMENT OF AMERICAN STUDIES
AMHERST COLLEGE

D. C. HEATH AND COMPANY: Boston

INTRODUCTION

THE Spanish-American War of 1898 and our subsequent annexation of the Philippines can no longer be viewed simply as quaint instances of American exuberance in the "gay" 1890's. Both the war and the act of expansion to which it led involved issues which have become primary concerns for twentieth-century Americans. The whole episode marked our emergence upon the international scene as one of the great powers. How well we understand the responsibilities of this comparatively new role may determine the very existence of American civilization.

The annexation of the Philippines which followed our defeat of Spain in the war brought a sharp divergence from previous American traditions. For the first time in our long history of territorial expansion we stepped beyond our continental limits to seize lands which lay much closer to the peoples of Asia than to our own shores. In every way the acquisition of these islands posed new problems for American civilization. Strategically we committed ourselves to defense of a remote outpost in the Far East. Politically we undertook to rule over millions of people who in all probability would never become full American citizens. Economically we hoped for promotion of our foreign trade through the aid of military force and political domination.

Here was one of the turning points in our history, and the debate from 1898 to 1900 over annexation of the Philippines constituted one of the great debates of American history. In a world where other great powers were rapidly absorbing the undeveloped portions of the globe, was it not both the duty and the interest of the United States to annex the Philippines? Failure to do so would leave the islands open to seizure by another power which might treat the natives with far greater harshness and which might use the islands to the detriment of American trade and security. Anti-imperialists, on the other hand, asked whether a republic like the United States could afford to contradict its political and social traditions by assuming control over other peoples who were to be its subjects, not its citizens. Would not such a course endanger our basic institutions and weaken our philosophy of government? These were the central and the enduring questions which posed the dilemma for thoughtful citizens. By 1899 the Senate had reached its decision to annex the Philippines. The reelection of President McKinley in 1900 seemed to indicate that the American people had no strong desire to repudiate this venture in imperialism.

How to explain the basic forces which led the United States into war and into expansion forms the primary problem raised in this volume. The secondary question posed by these readings is whether the decision for annexation was in the best national interest.

On April 19, 1898, Congress passed a resolution authorizing President McKinley to employ the armed forces of the United States to secure the independence of Cuba and the withdrawal of all Spanish control from that island. In addition, the Teller Amendment to this resolution disavowed any intention on the part of the United States to claim jurisdiction over Cuba once the Spaniards had been expelled. This Congressional action came as the climax to three years of agitation over the Cuban question. In 1895 the smoldering resentment of the Cubans at the harsh conditions of Spanish rule had burst forth into open rebellion. Guerrilla warfare, atrocities, concentration camps, and systematic destruction of property embittered the struggle on both sides. Many Americans sympathized with the Cuban desire for independence from an oppressive Old World empire. The United States government under both President Cleveland and President McKinley attempted through diplomatic channels to moderate and if possible to end the conflict while urging the Spaniards to grant some form of autonomy to Cuba. Despite continuing friction, relations between Spain and the United States had improved somewhat by the beginning of 1898 when two incidents occurred suddenly to inflame American passions against that country. The first of these was publication in a New York paper of the De Lôme letter, a private letter written by the Spanish Minister in the United States to a friend in Cuba in which the Minister described President McKinley as "weak and a bidder for the admiration of the crowd." Six days later a mysterious explosion sank the battleship *Maine* in the harbor of Havana killing 260 American officers and men. Historians generally agree that these two incidents precipitated the Congressional resolution which brought us into war with Spain.

These bare facts, however, scarcely seem a sufficient explanation for a declaration of war. This was not the first time there had been a rebellion in Cuba. From 1868 to 1878 the Cubans had engaged in a similar revolt against Spanish authority. During that conflict an incendiary incident had also occurred when Spanish officials seized on the high seas a ship flying the American flag and after a summary court martial executed fifty-three of its passengers and crew for aiding the rebels. Neither President Grant nor Congress asked for war at that time. As for the De Lôme letter, De Lôme resigned immediately upon publication of the letter. No government can be responsible for the private indiscretions of its diplomats, and Spain apologized promptly for her erring Minister. To this day no one knows the true cause for the explosion of the *Maine*. Spain had every reason to avoid instead of to promote such a catastrophe. She tendered her regrets to the United States and suggested that an impartial tribunal be appointed to investigate the explosion.

President McKinley sent his war message to Congress two days after Spain had declared the suspension of hostilities in Cuba and at a time when the able American Minister to Spain was advising the President that a satisfactory solution to the Cuban question could be peaceably achieved within a matter of months. Why the United States should have decided upon war under these circumstances obviously requires a more searching examination of basic forces and pressures within the nation.

It is no less puzzling to understand from the surface facts how a war to liberate the Cubans from Spanish imperialism could have been turned into an instrument for American imperialism in the Far East. The crucial connecting link, of

course, was Admiral Dewey's defeat of
the Spanish fleet at Manila. Presumably
this was a defensive measure taken to
prevent the Spaniards from attacking our
west coast. The truth is, though it may
well have been unknown to Americans at
that time, that the aged Spanish fleet at
Manila was in too wretched a condition
to attempt any forays across the Pacific.
Assuming, however, that Dewey and the
authorities in Washington believed the
destruction of that crippled fleet necessary to American security, it is still not
clear why Dewey did not sail away from
Manila once he had destroyed the fleet.
Why instead should he have requested
an army of occupation for the Philippines,
and why, above all, should President Mc-
Kinley have authorized the dispatch of
such an army within a few days of
Dewey's victory?

From the moment of Dewey's victory
in Manila Bay events and decisions seem
to have pyramided upon one another in
an almost irresistible fashion until the
final decision for annexation of the Philippines was made. In his instructions to
the American commissioners appointed
to negotiate the peace treaty McKinley
himself observed "the march of events
rules and overrules human action." Were
these simply a fortuitous series of accidents which led America into the path of
imperialism, or were there identifiable in-
fluences and specific human agents guiding the nation's course? Many contemporaries were convinced that all this was
a part of America's "manifest destiny,"
that an inscrutable Providence was at
work extending the blessings of American
civilization both into the Caribbean and
the Pacific. Richard Hofstadter has commented, however, ". . . where contemporaries heard the voice of God we think
we can discern the carnal larynx of Theodore Roosevelt." Other scholars would

substitute for Roosevelt's shrill tones as
the directing voice in national affairs
either the soft but weighty words of financiers and industrialists or the screaming
headlines of a William Randolph Hearst.

Some writers trace both the decision
for war and the decision for taking the
Philippines to the same sources. Others
find sharp differences between the major
groups supporting each of these steps,
with only a small minority group strongly
interested in both actions. All of the first
six authors in this collection, however
they may differ, are primarily concerned
with discovering the dominant factors at
work in this turning point of our history.

Probably the most influential single
study of imperialism was first published
by J. A. Hobson, an English economist,
over fifty years ago. From the 1938 edition of Hobson's classic work, *Imperialism, A Study,* the first reading selection is
taken. Unlike most other authors in this
volume, Hobson endeavors to survey the
phenomenon of imperialism in all the
leading countries of Europe at the close
of the nineteenth century as well as in the
United States. He finds a common "tap-
root" for the widespread surge of imperialism in the desire of financiers and
industrialists to secure profitable investments and markets for the rapidly accel-
erating accumulation of capital and consolidation of industry. His analysis deserves careful consideration not only for
its own logic and insight but also for the
influence which it has had. Drawing
largely upon Hobson's ideas, writers like
Hilferding and Lenin have extended the
Marxist analysis of capitalism to conclude
that imperialism is the final stage of capitalism which precedes and produces the
eventual collapse of capitalist society.
Both the foreign policy and the propaganda charges of Soviet Russia today are
strongly influenced by premises taken

from Lenin's *Imperialism, The Last Stage of Capitalism.*

In the second reading selection, Harvard's able diplomatic historian William L. Langer provides a thoughtful critique in which he contends that "the actual course of history refutes" Hobson's thesis. From his own extensive knowledge of European history during the period of imperialist expansion, Langer calls attention to the role of psychological and political factors in imperialism.

Focusing their examination directly on the American scene, the remaining authors, with one exception, tend to distinguish more sharply than Hobson between the causes for our war with Spain and the causes for our imperialism in the Pacific. That one exception is the historian Charles A. Beard, who discusses both topics under the heading of "Territorial Expansion Connected with Commerce" and who dismisses any "fortuitous aspects" in the events which ended with annexation of the Philippines. While recognizing our strategic interests in Cuba, Beard lays heavy emphasis upon economic interests and the plans of militarists behind our decisions.

The next article, "American Business and the Spanish-American War" by Julius W. Pratt, is an attempt to ascertain from the public statements of business journals and from other sources exactly what were the opinions of American financiers and industrialists toward the war with Spain and the annexation of the Philippines. The findings of this noted diplomatic historian did much to revise previous explanations of the war and to separate the motivations for war from the motivations for expansion. Following the publication of Pratt's article, Joseph E. Wisan concentrated attention upon the influence of sensationalist newspapers in stirring up a popular clamor for war. The selections

here included from Wisan's extensive study of *The Cuban Crisis as Reflected in the New York Press* support his conclusion that the circulation race between the *New York World* and the *New York Journal* provided the indispensable element in causation of the war.

Not wholly content with any of these explanations, Richard Hofstadter has recently analyzed this turning point in our history from a somewhat different perspective. As an historian with a keen interest in such allied disciplines as sociology and social psychology, he contends that the war and the Philippines venture cannot properly be understood without taking account of what he calls "the psychic crisis of the 1890's." His essay examines those psychological and political factors which Langer suggests are important in imperialism.

Selections from four authors who differ vigorously over the wisdom of the decision to annex the Philippines conclude this volume. One of the leading contemporary proponents of the expansionist policy, Henry Cabot Lodge, argues in a Senate speech that annexation is both the duty and the interest of the United States. As a prominent spokesman for the Anti-Imperialist League in 1899, Carl Schurz replies that such a step runs counter to the best traditions and the best interests of the nation. Later historians have continued the sharp debate. While Samuel F. Bemis considers our extension into the Far East to have been "The Great Aberration," another historian, Tyler Dennett, concludes that by remaining in the Philippines we followed the only feasible course at that time.

In a recent book, *American Diplomacy, 1900–1950*, George F. Kennan has undertaken to investigate "the basic concepts underlying the conduct of the external relations of the United States." This thoughtful diplomat, who before his re- tirement was head of the State Depart- ment's Policy Planning Staff and then our Ambassador to Russia, begins his exam- ination with a chapter on our war with Spain. Summarizing the crucial questions over which Americans differed in 1898, he concludes:

Let us content ourselves with recording that in the course of their deliberations they stum- bled upon issues and problems basic to the health of our American civilization; that these issues and problems are ones which are still before us and still require answer; and that, whereas the men of 1898 could afford to be mistaken in their answers to them, our gener- ation no longer has this luxury.

CONTENTS

OPENING OF THE FISHING SEASON. UNCLE
SAM SEEMS TO BE MAKING A GOOD CATCH.
— *The Journal, Minneapolis*

HOW SOME APPREHENSIVE PEOPLE PICTURE
UNCLE SAM AFTER THE WAR.
— *The News, Detroit*

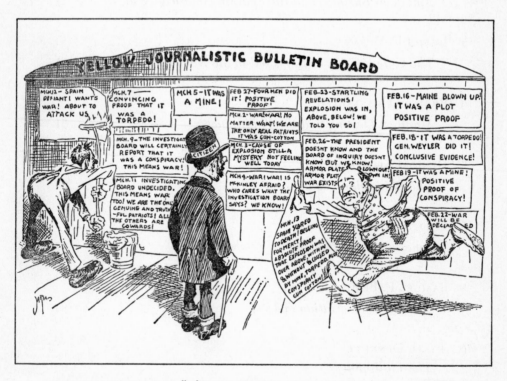

THE PATIENT CITIZEN — "IT'S VERY CONFUSING BUT POSSIBLY IT'S ALL TRUE."
— *The Record, Chicago*

The Clash of Issues

Scholars disagree on the role of economic factors in imperialism:

". . . whereas various real and powerful motives of pride, prestige and pugnacity, together with the more altruistic professions of a civilising mission, figured as causes of imperial expansion, the dominant directive motive was the demand for markets and for profitable investment by the exporting and financial classes within each imperialist régime."

— JOHN A. HOBSON

"But in going all out for the theory that man's actions can be traced to the fact of his dependence on material things, the new interpreters of history went too far . . . and forgot that the pursuit of power can arise from a number of causes in which economic motives play no evident or conceivable part. . . . And those familiar stand-bys of the history books (which generally are given a place considerably below the economic factors) — love of adventure, prestige ('face'), strategy, civilizing missions, and political and ideological clashes — have certainly been potent causes of imperialism and war."

— EARL M. WINSLOW

Historians differ on the power of the press:

"In the opinion of the writer, the Spanish-American War would not have occurred had not the appearance of Hearst in New York journalism precipitated a bitter battle for newspaper circulation."

— JOSEPH E. WISAN

"The alternative explanation has been the equally simple idea that the war was a newspapers' war. . . . [but] the press itself, whatever it can do with opinion, does not have the power to precipitate opinion into action. . . . We must, then, supplement our story about the role of the newspapers with at least two other factors: the state of the public temper upon which the newspapers worked, and the manner in which party rivalries deflected domestic clashes into foreign aggression."

— RICHARD HOFSTADTER

Contemporaries debated the wisdom of American imperialism:

"Thus . . . duty and interest alike, duty of the highest kind and interest of the highest and best kind, impose upon us the retention of the Philippines, the development of the islands, and the expansion of our Eastern commerce."

— HENRY CABOT LODGE

"A self-governing state cannot accept sovereignty over an unwilling people. The United States cannot act upon the ancient heresy that might makes right."

— PLATFORM OF ANTI-IMPERIALIST LEAGUE IN 1899

The statement by E. M. Winslow is from *The Pattern of Imperialism* (New York: Columbia University Press, 1948), 67. Reprinted by permission.

J. A. Hobson: IMPERIALISM

INTRODUCTION TO THE 1938 EDITION

... IT may be convenient here to rehearse in bare terms the main argument of this book, and then to discuss such changes and modifications of the earlier argument as the current of recent history appears to demand.

That argument was to the effect that whereas various real and powerful motives of pride, prestige and pugnacity, together with the more altruistic professions of a civilising mission, figured as causes of imperial expansion, the dominant directive motive was the demand for markets and for profitable investment by the exporting and financial classes within each imperialist régime. The urgency of this economic demand was attributed to the growing tendency of industrial productivity, under the new capitalist technique of machinery and power, to exceed the effective demand of the national markets, the rate of production to outrun the rate of home consumption. This was not, of course, the whole story. The rising productivity of industry required larger imports of some forms of raw materials, more imported foods for larger urban populations, and a great variety of imported consumption goods for a rising standard of living. These imports could only be purchased by a corresponding expansion of exports, or else by the incomes derived from foreign investments which implied earlier exports of capital goods.

But with these qualifications in mind,

it is nevertheless true that the most potent drive towards enlarged export trade was the excess of capitalist production over the demands of the home market. ...

My contention is that the system prevailing in all developed countries for the production and distribution of wealth has reached a stage in which its productive powers are held in leash by its inequalities of distribution; the excessive share that goes to profits, rents and other surpluses impelling a chronic endeavour to oversave in the sense of trying to provide an increased productive power without a corresponding outlet in the purchase of consumable goods. This drive towards oversaving is gradually checked by the inability of such saving to find any profitable use in the provision of more plant and other capital. But it also seeks to utilise political power for outlets in external markets, and as foreign independent markets are closed or restricted, the drive to the acquisition of colonies, protectorates and other areas of imperial development becomes a more urgent and conscious national policy. If this reasoning is correct, capitalism to maintain its profitable character, by utilising its new productive powers as fully as possible, is impelled to seek the help of the State in the various ways that are now so much in evidence, tariffs, embargoes, subsidies, and the acquisition or retention of colonies where the home capitalist can have advantages both for his import and export

From J. A. Hobson, *Imperialism* (London: George Allen and Unwin Ltd., 1938), pp. v–vi, xii–xiii, xvii–xxii, 55–61, 71–81. Used by permission.

trade, with such securities in monetary matters as can be provided by imperial control. . . .

But there remains a wider issue for our consideration. Suppose it to be the case that the education of the workers in most capitalist countries has been bringing into the forefront of their consciousness the injustices, the wastes, the cruelties of the current economic system in its effects on the production and distribution of wealth. Suppose some demand for a new economic system that shall displace the imperfectly competitive capitalism, and shall organise the available human and material resources of production on a conscious basis of the satisfaction of human needs — suppose that such a demand is visibly seeking expression through the democratic machinery of popular self-government, is it not reasonable to expect that strong capitalist interests would seek methods of repressing these thoughts and designs of the workers?

For though capitalism might hope to maintain some of its supremacy by such concessions to labour and such extensions of social services as would buy off the organised resentment of the workers, the results of such a concession policy might be inadequate to meet the actual economic pressure. For the larger working class and public consumption involved in this policy might be conducive to an increased efficiency of labour and advance of productive technique great enough to keep capitalism upon a basis so profitable that the disequilibrium between production and consumption continues as a disturbing influence in industry. This issue of the sufficiency of this concession policy is, indeed, being worked out in Britain to-day, and the United States is making some attempt at its application in America. Its success would seem to imply a formal retention of capitalism as the di-

rective power of industry, working in closely organized relations with the employees in the several industries and the consumer as the coordinative factor in the relations of the several industries. Some such alteration in the form and functions of capitalism is also apparent in the Italian and the German schemes for a Corporative State. But in all these cases of public planning two difficulties have to be confronted. First, the question how far large personal gains are a necessary stimulus to the creative work of men responsible for rapid and advantageous improvements in technique and organization. Routine workers necessarily tend to overlook the enormous productive importance of such creative activities, or to think that they can always be secured by departments of technical research attached to each industry. It may, therefore, be desirable to leave outside any scheme of public planning those newer industries where rapid improvements of technique may be expected and those industries most susceptible to changes in the demand for the goods they supply.

But important as this question may be of securing the best inventive and administrative services by adequate incentives of gain, there remains another question of still greater importance, viz. the utilization or the displacement of that financial control over big industry which is the latest fruit of capitalist evolution. The closest study of this financial control has been made by the American economist Thorstein Veblen who examines the relations which exist in the United States between the manipulations of credit and prices and the industrial management. Whereas the latter aims at the highest technical and working efficiency in producing the maximum output, the former pay exclusive regard to the regulation and limitation of that output so as to maintain a price level which shall yield the largest aggregate profit. In many standard industries for the production of the necessaries and conventional comforts of life, it may pay the financiers and investors to market a limited quantity of goods at a higher price. Hence the tendency of the bankers and other organizers of finance to promote cartels, trusts and other amalgamations which shall enable them to control the aggregate output, closing down superfluous plants and reducing the volume of employment. Though America with her highly organized money-power and her protective system has taken the lead in this financial dominion, other capitalist countries, Germany and Britain in particular, have made considerable advances in the same direction. In Germany the banks have for a long time past devoted themselves to these profitable restrictions of industry, and more recently the textile, metal, mining, milling and other standard industries in Great Britain have been seeking similar organization for the profitable regulation of output.

This analysis of the various attempts to escape from the perils of excessive productivity shows that they fall under three heads. One consists in the policy of organized labour and the State, aiming to secure a more equal and equitable distribution of the money and real income of the community, by higher wages, shorter hours and other betterment of working and living conditions. The second consists in the business policy of restricted output just described, involving a close financial control of the major businesses in specified national or international industries, accompanied by a regulation of their markets and, when deemed desirable, by quotas and tariffs. The third method, and that most relevant to our present subject of Imperialism, is the combined or separate action of capital to obtain the help, financial, diplomatic, military, of the national government so as to secure preferential access to foreign markets and foreign areas of development by colonies, protectorates, spheres of preferential trade and other methods of a pushful economic foreign policy. It may be true that the people of the imperialist state are in the long, or even the short, run losers by a policy so costly in money and in lives. But if, as is normally the case, the larger part of this expense falls upon the public as a whole, it may still be advantageous to those capitalist interests engaged in foreign trade and investments to promote a policy that is to their profit. Even if, as Sir Norman Angell contends, such imperialism involves war-making and with it the perils of a domestic revolution fatal to the capitalist régime, the risks of such an issue may either be unrealised, or may be disregarded in view of the immediate gains which imperialism brings to favoured industries. If, as many close investigators of the business world appear to hold, the capitalism which has prevailed for the past few centuries is in any case destined to disappear, it may seem better for its defenders to endeavour to prolong its life by political pressure for external markets than to succumb without a struggle to the popular demand for state socialism or a policy of social services, the expenses of which shall consume the whole of surplus profits. There still remain large fields for capitalist exploitation. The largest of these, China, appears to be marked down for Japanese exclusive exploitation. But this appearance is deceptive, for the task of Chinese development far exceeds the national resources of Japan. If capitalists in the several Western Powers were capable of intelligent co-operation, instead of wrangling among themselves for separate national areas of exploitation, they would have combined for a joint international enterprise in Asia, a project which might have given the whole of Western capitalism another generation of active profitable survival. Such a scheme of economic Interimperialism may now no longer be possible, for though Japan cannot perform her self-imposed task without financial assistance from the wealthier West, she may be able to obtain this assistance by making the financiers of several Western countries compete with one another for the provision of the required finance, without allowing their governments any real share in the accompanying political control over China.

From the standpoint of the defence of capitalism it is not necessary to show that imperialism is profitable in the long run to the general body of the owning and exploiting class within a capitalist country, but only that it enables the members of that class concerned with foreign trade and investment to utilize the political and financial resources of their State to extend the area of such trade and investment or to retain and develop the colonies, protectorates and other portions of the existing empire.

It is such considerations that bring out the conflict of imperialism with democracy. For a political democracy, in which the interests and will of the whole people wield the powers of the State, will actively oppose the whole process of imperialism. Such a democracy has now learnt the lesson that substantial economic equality in income and ownership of property is essential to its operation. The defence of capitalism is, therefore, bound up in every country with the destruction or enfeeblement of the popular franchise and representative government. If the forms of such democracy are still retained, they are reduced to the automatic or compulsory registration of the will of a dictator or a ruling caste. The cases above cited suffice to show the place which Imperialism occupies as an ingredient in the capitalist-military nationalism of the age. There is, of course, some division of interest and policy between the military rulers who in Japan, as in Germany, conduct the territorial aggressions, and the capitalists who must help to finance them. But the clearer-sighted capitalists perceive that dictatorship and their imperial enterprises, expensive as they may be, are preferable to the more revolutionary courses to which democracies are now committed. Imperialism thus figures as an important and imposing feature of neo-capitalism, seeking to avert internal democratic struggles for economic equalitarianism by providing outlets for surplus goods and surplus population together with emotional appeals to the combatant predacity which animates a spirited foreign policy. It may be true that Imperialism in its competitive aspect carries within itself the seeds of its own demise, leading, as it must, to conflicts ever more destructive to life and property. Indeed, its competition for an ever shrinking area of profitable acquisition may so intensify the struggle between the possessing and the non-possessing nations as to destroy the fabric of civilization. Whether the slowly evolving rationality and sociability of man have advanced sufficiently to furnish a strong enough safeguard against this imperial predacity is the question that confronts the world to-day. . . .

THE ECONOMIC PARASITES OF IMPERIALISM

Aggressive Imperialism, which costs the taxpayer so dear, which is of so little value to the manufacturer and trader, which is fraught with such grave incalculable peril to the citizen, is a source of great gain to the investor who cannot find at home the profitable use he seeks for his capital, and insists that his Government should help him to profitable and secure investments abroad.

If, contemplating the enormous expenditure on armaments, the ruinous wars, the diplomatic audacity or knavery by which modern Governments seek to extend their territorial power, we put the plain, practical question, *Cui bono?* the first and most obvious answer is, the investor.

The annual income Great Britain derives from commissions on her whole foreign and colonial trade, import and export, was estimated by Sir R. Giffen at £18,000,000 for 1899, taken at 2½ per cent., upon a turnover of £800,000,000. This is the whole that we are entitled to regard as profits on external trade. Considerable as this sum is, it cannot serve to yield an economic motive-power adequate to explain the dominance which business considerations exercise over our imperial policy. Only when we set beside it some £90,000,000 or £100,000,000, representing pure profit upon investments, do we understand whence the economic impulse to Imperialism is derived.

Investors who have put their money in foreign lands, upon terms which take full account of risks connected with the political conditions of the country, desire to use the resources of their Government to minimise these risks, and so to enhance the capital value and the interest of their private investments. The investing and speculative classes in general have also desired that Great Britain should take other foreign areas under her flag in order to secure new areas for profitable investments and speculation.

If the special interest of the investor is liable to clash with the public interest and to induce a wrecking policy, still more dangerous is the special interest of the financier, the general dealer in investments. In large measure the rank and file of the investors are, both for business and for politics, the cat'spaws of the great financial houses, who use stocks and shares not so much as investments to yield them interest, but as material for speculation in the money market. In handling large masses of stocks and shares, in floating companies, in manipulating fluctuations of values, the magnates of the Bourse find their gain. These great businesses — banking, broking, bill discounting, loan floating, company promoting— form the central ganglion of international capitalism. United by the strongest bonds of organisation, always in closest and quickest touch with one another, situated in the very heart of the business capital of every State, controlled, so far as Europe is concerned, chiefly by men of a single and peculiar race, who have behind them many centuries of financial experience, they are in a unique position to manipulate the policy of nations. No great quick direction of capital is possible save by their consent and through their agency. Does any one seriously suppose that a great war could be undertaken by any European State, or a great State loan subscribed, if the house of Rothschild and its connexions set their face against it?

Every great political act involving a new flow of capital, or a large fluctuation in the values of existing investments, must receive the sanction and the practical aid of this little group of financial kings. These men, holding their realised wealth and their business capital, as they must, chiefly in stocks and bonds, have a double stake, first as investors, but secondly and chiefly as financial dealers. As investors, their political influence does not differ essentially from that of the smaller investors, except that they usually possess a practical control of the businesses in which they invest. As speculators or financial dealers they constitute, however, the gravest single factor in the economics of Imperialism.

To create new public debts, to float new companies, and to cause constant considerable fluctuations of values are three conditions of their profitable business. Each condition carries them into politics, and throws them on the side of Imperialism.

The public financial arrangements for the Philippine war put several millions of dollars into the pockets of Mr. Pierpont Morgan and his friends; the China-Japan war, which saddled the Celestial Empire for the first time with a public debt, and the indemnity which she will pay to her European invaders in connexion with the recent conflict, bring grist to the financial mills in Europe; every railway or mining concession wrung from some reluctant foreign potentate means profitable business in raising capital and floating companies. A policy which rouses fears of aggression in Asiatic states, and which fans the rivalry of commercial nations in Europe, evokes vast expenditure on armaments, and ever-accumulating public debts, while the doubts and risks accruing from this policy promote that constant oscillation of values of securities which is so profitable to the skilled financier. There is not a war, a revolution, an anarchist assassination, or any other public shock, which is not gainful to these men; they

are harpies who suck their gains from every new forced expenditure and every sudden disturbance of public credit. To the financiers "in the know" the Jameson raid was a most advantageous coup, as may be ascertained by a comparison of the "holdings" of these men before and after that event; the terrible sufferings of England and South Africa in the war, which was a sequel of the raid, has been a source of immense profit to the big financiers who have best held out against the uncalculated waste, and have recouped themselves by profitable war contracts and by "freezing out" the smaller interests in the Transvaal. These men are the only certain gainers from the war, and most of their gains are made out of the public losses of their adopted country or the private losses of their fellow-countrymen.

The policy of these men, it is true, does not necessarily make for war; where war would bring about too great and too permanent a damage to the substantial fabric of industry, which is the ultimate and essential basis of speculation, their influence is cast for peace, as in the dangerous quarrel between Great Britain and the United States regarding Venezuela. But every increase of public expenditure, every oscillation of public credit short of this collapse, every risky enterprise in which public resources can be made the pledge of private speculations, is profitable to the big money-lender and speculator.

The wealth of these houses, the scale of their operations, and their cosmopolitan organisation make them the prime determinants of imperial policy. They have the largest definite stake in the business of Imperialism, and the amplest means of forcing their will upon the policy of nations.

In view of the part which the noneconomic factors of patriotism, adventure, military enterprise, political ambition, and philanthropy play in imperial expansion, it may appear that to impute to financiers so much power is to take a too narrowly economic view of history. And it is true that the motor-power of Imperialism is not chiefly financial: finance is rather the governor of the imperial engine, directing the energy and determining its work: it does not constitute the fuel of the engine, nor does it directly generate the power. Finance manipulates the patriotic forces which politicians, soldiers, philanthropists, and traders generate; the enthusiasm for expansion which issues from these sources, though strong and genuine, is irregular and blind; the financial interest has those qualities of concentration and clear-sighted calculation which are needed to set Imperialism to work. An ambitious statesman, a frontier soldier, an overzealous missionary, a pushing trader, may suggest or even initiate a step of imperial expansion, may assist in educating patriotic public opinion to the urgent need of some fresh advance, but the final determination rests with the financial power. The direct influence exercised by great financial houses in "high politics" is supported by the control which they exercise over the body of public opinion through the Press, which, in every "civilized" country, is becoming more and more their obedient instrument. While the specifically financial newspaper imposes "facts" and "opinions" on the business classes, the general body of the Press comes more and more under the conscious or unconscious domination of financiers. The case of the South African Press, whose agents and correspondents fanned the martial flames in this country, was one of open ownership on the part of South African financiers, and this policy of owning newspapers for the sake of manufacturing public opinion is common in the great European cities. In Berlin, Vienna, and Paris many of the influential newspapers have been held by financial houses, which used them, not primarily to make direct profits out of them, but in order to put into the public mind beliefs and sentiments which would influence public policy and thus affect the money market. In Great Britain this policy has not gone so far, but the alliance with finance grows closer every year, either by financiers purchasing a controlling share of newspapers, or by newspaper proprietors being tempted into finance. Apart from the financial Press, and financial ownership of the general Press, the City has notoriously exercised a subtle and abiding influence upon leading London newspapers, and through them upon the body of the provincial Press, while the entire dependence of the Press for its business profits upon its advertising columns has involved a peculiar reluctance to oppose the organised financial classes with whom rests the control of so much advertising business. Add to this the natural sympathy with a sensational policy which a cheap Press always manifests, and it becomes evident that the Press has been strongly biased towards Imperialism, and has lent itself with great facility to the suggestion of financial or political Imperialists who have desired to work up patriotism for some new piece of expansion.

Such is the array of distinctively economic forces making for Imperialism, a large loose group of trades and professions seeking profitable business and lucrative employment from the expansion of military and civil services, and from the expenditure on military operations, the opening up of new tracts of territory and trade with the same, and the provision of new capital which these operations require, all these finding their central guiding and directing force in the power of the general financier.

The play of these forces does not openly appear. They are essentially parasites upon patriotism, and they adapt themselves to its protecting colours. In the mouth of their representatives are noble phrases, expressive of their desire to extend the area of civilisation, to establish good government, promote Christianity, extirpate slavery, and elevate the lower races. Some of the business men who hold such language may entertain a genuine, though usually a vague, desire to accomplish these ends, but they are primarily engaged in business, and they are not unaware of the utility of the more unselfish forces in furthering their ends. Their true attitude of mind was expressed by Mr. Rhodes in his famous description of "Her Majesty's Flag" as "the greatest commercial asset in the world.". . .

THE ECONOMIC TAPROOT OF IMPERIALISM

No mere array of facts and figures adduced to illustrate the economic nature of the new Imperialism will suffice to dispel the popular delusion that the use of national force to secure new markets by annexing fresh tracts of territory is a sound and a necessary policy for an advanced industrial country like Great Britain. It has indeed been proved that recent annexations of tropical countries, procured at great expense, have furnished poor and precarious markets, that our aggregate trade with our colonial possessions is virtually stationary, and that our most profitable and progressive trade is with rival industrial nations, whose territories we have no desire to annex, whose markets we cannot force, and whose active antagonism we are provoking by our expansive policy.

But these arguments are not conclusive. It is open to Imperialists to argue this: "We must have markets for our growing manufactures, we must have new outlets for the investment of our surplus capital and for the energies of the adventurous surplus of our population: such expansion is a necessity of life to a nation with our great and growing powers of production. An ever larger share of our population is devoted to the manufactures and commerce of towns, and is thus dependent for life and work upon food and raw materials from foreign lands. In order to buy and pay for these things we must sell our goods abroad. During the first three-quarters of the nineteenth century we could do so without difficulty by a natural expansion of commerce with continental nations and our colonies, all of which were far behind us in the main arts of manufacture and the carrying trades. So long as England held a virtual monopoly of the world markets for certain important classes of manufactured goods, Imperialism was unnecessary. After 1870 this manufacturing and trading supremacy was greatly impaired: other nations, especially Germany, the United States, and Belgium, advanced with great rapidity, and while they have not crushed or even stayed the increase of our external trade, their competition made it more and more difficult to dispose of the full surplus of our manufactures at a profit. The encroachments made by these nations upon our old markets, even in our own possessions, made it most urgent that we should take energetic means to secure new markets. These new markets had to lie in hitherto undeveloped countries, chiefly in the tropics, where vast populations lived capable of growing economic needs which our manufacturers and merchants could supply. Our rivals were seizing and annexing territories for similar purposes, and when they had annexed them closed them to our trade. The diplomacy and the arms of Great Britain had to be used in order to compel the owners of the new markets to deal with us: and experience showed that the safest means of securing and developing such markets is by establishing 'protectorates' or by annexation. The value in 1905 of these markets must not be taken as a final test of the economy of such a policy; the process of educating civilized needs which we can supply is of necessity a gradual one, and the cost of such Imperialism must be regarded as a capital outlay, the fruits of which posterity would reap. The new markets might not be large, but they formed serviceable outlets for the overflow of our great textile and metal industries, and, when the vast Asiatic and African populations of the interior were reached, a rapid expansion of trade was expected to result.

"Far larger and more important is the pressure of capital for external fields of investment. Moreover, while the manufacturer and trader are well content to trade with foreign nations, the tendency for investors to work towards the political annexation of countries which contain their more speculative investments is very powerful. Of the fact of this pressure of capital there can be no question. Large savings are made which cannot find any profitable investment in this country; they must find employment elsewhere, and it is to the advantage of the nation that they should be employed as largely as possible in lands where they can be utilized in opening up markets for British trade and employment for British enterprise.

"However costly, however perilous, this process of imperial expansion may be, it is necessary to the continued existence and progress of our nation; if we abandoned it we must be content to leave the development of the world to other nations, who will everywhere cut into our trade, and even impair our means of securing the food and raw materials we require to support our population. Imperialism is thus seen to be, not a choice, but a necessity."

The practical force of this economic argument in politics is strikingly illustrated by the later history of the United States. Here is a country which suddenly broke through a conservative policy, strongly held by both political parties, bound up with every popular instinct and tradition, and flung itself into a rapid imperial career for which it possessed neither the material nor the moral equipment, risking the principles and practices of liberty and equality by the establishment of militarism and the forcible subjugation of peoples which it could not safely admit to the condition of American citizenship.

Was this a mere wild freak of spread-eaglism, a burst of political ambition on the part of a nation coming to a sudden realization of its destiny? Not at all. The spirit of adventure, the American "mission of civilization," were as forces making for Imperialism, clearly subordinate to the driving force of the economic factor. The dramatic character of the change is due to the unprecedented rapidity of the industrial revolution in the United States from the eighties onwards. During that period the United States, with her unrivalled natural resources, her immense resources of skilled and unskilled labour, and her genius for invention and organization, developed the best equipped and most productive manufacturing economy the world has yet seen. Fostered by rigid protective tariffs, her metal, textile, tool, clothing, furniture, and other manufactures shot up in a single generation from infancy to full maturity, and, having passed through a period of intense competition, attained, under the able control of great trust-makers, a power of production greater than has been attained in the most advanced industrial countries of Europe.

An era of cut-throat competition, followed by a rapid process of amalgamation, threw an enormous quantity of wealth into the hands of a small number of captains of industry. No luxury of living to which this class could attain kept pace with its rise of income, and a process of automatic saving set in upon an unprecedented scale. The investment of these savings in other industries helped to bring these under the same concentrative forces. Thus a great increase of savings seeking profitable investment is synchronous with a stricter economy of the use of existing capital. No doubt the rapid growth of a population, accustomed to a high and an always ascending standard of comfort, absorbs in the satisfaction of its wants a large quantity of new capital. But the actual rate of saving, conjoined with a more economical application of forms of existing capital, exceeded considerably the rise of the national consumption of manufactures. The power of production far outstripped the actual rate of consumption, and, contrary to the older economic theory, was unable to force a corresponding increase of consumption by lowering prices.

This is no mere theory. The history of any of the numerous trusts or combinations in the United States sets out the facts with complete distinctness. In the free competition of manufactures preceding combination the chronic condition is one of "over-production," in the sense that all the mills or factories can only be kept at work by cutting prices down towards a point where the weaker competitors are forced to close down, because they cannot sell their goods at a price which covers the true cost of production. The first result of the successful formation of a trust or combine is to close down the worse equipped or worse placed mills, and supply the entire market from the better equipped and better placed ones. This course may or may not be attended by a rise of price and some restriction of consumption: in some cases trusts take most of their profits by raising prices, in other cases by reducing the costs of production through employing only the best mills and stopping the waste of competition.

For the present argument it matters not which course is taken; the point is that this concentration of industry in "trusts," "combines," etc., at once limits the quantity of capital which can be effectively employed and increases the share of profits out of which fresh savings and fresh capital will spring. It is quite evident that a trust which is motived by cut-throat competition, due to an excess of capital, cannot normally find inside the "trusted" industry employment for that portion of the profits which the trust-makers desire to save and to invest. New inventions and other economies of production or distribution within the trade may absorb some of the new capital, but there are rigid limits to this absorption. The trust-maker in oil or sugar must find other investments for his savings: if he is early in the application of the combination principles to his trade, he will naturally apply his surplus capital to establish similar combinations in other industries, economising capital still further, and rendering it ever harder for ordinary saving men to find investments for their savings.

Indeed, the conditions alike of cut-throat competition and of combination attest the congestion of capital in the manufacturing industries which have entered the machine economy. We are not here concerned with any theoretic question as to the possibility of producing by modern machine methods more goods than can find a market. It is sufficient to point out that the manufacturing power of a country like the United States would grow so fast as to exceed the demands of the home market. No one acquainted with trade will deny a fact which all American economists assert, that this is the condition which the United States reached at the end of the century, so far as the more developed industries are concerned. Her manufactures were saturated with capital and could absorb no more. One after another they sought refuge from the waste of competition in "combines" which secure a measure of profitable peace by restricting the quantity of operative capital. Industrial and financial princes in oil, steel, sugar, railroads, banking, etc., were faced with the dilemma of either spending more than they knew how to spend, or forcing markets outside the home area. Two economic courses were open to them, both leading towards an abandonment of the political isolation of the past and the adoption of imperialist methods in the future. Instead of shutting down inferior mills and rigidly restricting output to correspond with profitable sales in the home markets, they might employ their full productive power, applying their savings to increase their business capital, and, while still regulating output and prices for the home market, may "hustle" for foreign markets, dumping down their surplus goods at prices which would not be possible save for the profitable nature of their home market. So likewise they might employ their savings in seeking investments outside their country, first repaying the capital borrowed from Great Britain and other countries for the early development of their railroads, mines and manufactures, and afterwards becoming themselves a creditor class to foreign countries.

It was this sudden demand for foreign markets for manufactures and for investments which was avowedly responsible for the adoption of Imperialism as a political policy and practice by the Republican party to which the great industrial and financial chiefs belonged, and which belonged to them. The adventurous enthusiasm of President Theodore Roosevelt and his "manifest destiny" and "mission of civilization" party must not deceive us. It was Messrs. Rockefeller, Pierpont Morgan, and their associates who needed Imperialism and who fastened it upon the shoulders of the great Republic of the West. They needed Imperialism because they desired to use the public resources of their country to find profitable employment for their capital which otherwise would be superfluous.

It is not indeed necessary to own a country in order to do trade with it or to invest capital in it, and doubtless the United States could find some vent for their surplus goods and capital in European countries. But these countries were for the most part able to make provision for themselves: most of them erected tariffs against manufacturing imports, and even Great Britain was urged to defend herself by reverting to Protection. The big American manufacturers and financiers were compelled to look to China and the Pacific and to South America for their most profitable chances; Protectionists by principle and practice, they would insist upon getting as close a monopoly of these markets as they could secure, and the competition of Germany, England, and other trading nations would drive them to the establishment of special political relations with the markets they most prize. Cuba, the Philippines, and Hawaii were but the *hors d'oeuvre* to whet an appetite for an ampler banquet. Moreover, the powerful hold upon politics which these industrial and financial magnates possessed formed a separate stimulus, which, as we have shown, was operative in Great Britain and elsewhere; the public expenditure in pursuit of an imperial career would be a separate immense source of profit by these men, as financiers negotiating loans, shipbuilders and owners handling subsidies, contractors and manufacturers of armaments and other imperialist appliances.

The suddenness of this political revolution is due to the rapid manifestation of the need. In the last years of the nineteenth century the United States nearly trebled the value of its manufacturing export trade, and it was to be expected that, if the rate of progress of those years continued, within a decade it would overtake our more slowly advancing export trade, and stand first in the list of manufacture-exporting nations.

This was the avowed ambition, and no idle one, of the keenest business men of America; and with the natural resources, the labour and the administrative talents at their disposal, it was quite likely they would achieve their object. The stronger and more direct control over politics exercised in America by business men enabled them to drive more quickly and more straightly along the line of their economic interests than in Great Britain. American Imperialism was the natural product of the economic pressure of a sudden advance of capitalism which could not find occupation at home and needed foreign markets for goods and for investments.

Export Trade of United States, 1890–1900

Year	Agriculture	Manufactures	Miscellaneous
	£	£	£
1890	125,756,000	31,435,000	13,019,000
1891	146,617,000	33,720,000	11,731,000
1892	142,508,000	30,479,000	11,660,000
1893	123,810,000	35,484,000	11,653,000
1894	114,737,000	35,557,000	11,168,000
1895	104,143,000	40,230,000	12,174,000
1896	132,992,000	50,738,000	13,639,000
1897	146,059,000	55,923,000	13,984,000
1898	170,383,000	61,585,000	14,743,000
1899	156,427,000	76,157,000	18,002,000
1900	180,931,000	88,281,000	21,389,000

The same needs existed in European countries, and, as is admitted, drove Governments along the same path. Overproduction in the sense of an excessive manufacturing plant, and surplus capital which could not find sound investments within the country, forced Great Britain, Germany, Holland, France to place larger and larger portions of their economic resources outside the area of their present political domain, and then stimulate a policy of political expansion so as to take in the new areas. The economic sources of this movement are laid bare by periodic trade-depressions due to an inability of producers to find adequate and profitable markets for what they can produce. The Majority Report of the Commission upon the Depression of Trade in 1885 put the matter in a nutshell. "That, owing to the nature of the times, the demand for our commodities does not increase at the same rate as formerly; that our capacity for production is consequently in excess of our requirements, and could be considerably increased at short notice; that this is due partly to the competition of the capital which is being steadily accumulated in the country." The Minority Report straightly imputed the condition of affairs to "over-production." Germany was in the early 1900's suffering severely from what is called a glut of capital and of manufacturing power: she had to have new markets; her Consuls all over the world were "hustling" for trade; trading settlements were forced upon Asia Minor; in East and West Africa, in China and elsewhere the German Empire was impelled to a policy of colonization and protectorates as outlets for German commercial energy.

Every improvement of methods of production, every concentration of ownership and control, seems to accentuate the tendency. As one nation after another enters the machine economy and adopts advanced industrial methods, it becomes more difficult for its manufacturers, merchants, and financiers to dispose profitably of their economic resources, and they are tempted more and more to use their Governments in order to secure for their particular use some distant undeveloped country by annexation and protection....

William L. Langer:
A CRITIQUE OF IMPERIALISM

IT is now roughly fifty years since the beginning of that great outburst of expansive activity on the part of the Great Powers of Europe which we have come to call "imperialism." And it is about a generation since J. A. Hobson published his "Imperialism: a Study," a book which has served as the starting point for most later discussions and which has proved a perennial inspiration for writers of the most diverse schools. A reappraisal of it is therefore decidedly in order. The wonder is that it has not been undertaken sooner.

Since before the outbreak of the World War the theoretical writing on imperialism has been very largely monopolized by the so-called Neo-Marxians, that is, by those who, following in the footsteps of the master, have carried on his historical analysis from the critique of capitalism to the study of this further phase, imperialism, the significance of which Marx himself did not appreciate and the very existence of which he barely adumbrated. The Neo-Markians, beginning with Rudolf Hilferding and Rosa Luxemburg, have by this time elaborated a complete theory, which has recently been expounded in several ponderous German works. The theory hinges upon the idea of the accumulation of capital, its adherents holding that imperialism is nothing more nor less than the last stage in the development of capitalism — the stage in which the surplus capital resulting from the system of production is obliged by ever diminishing returns at home to seek new fields for investment abroad. When this surplus capital has transformed the whole world and remade even the most backward areas in the image of capitalism, the whole economic-social system will inevitably die of congestion.

That the classical writers of the socialistic school derived this basic idea from

From William L. Langer, "A Critique of Imperialism," *Foreign Affairs*, XIV, (October, 1935), 102–114. Used by permission.

Hobson's book there can be no doubt.[1] Lenin himself admitted, in his "Imperialism, the Latest Stage of Capitalism," that Hobson gave "a very good and accurate description of the fundamental economic and political traits of imperialism," and that Hobson and Hilferding had said the essentials on the subject. This, then, has been the most fruitful contribution of Hobson's essay. When we examine his ideas on this subject we refer indirectly to the larger part of the writing on imperialism since his day.

As a matter of pure economic theory it is most difficult to break down the logic of the accumulation theory. It is a fact that since the middle of the last century certain countries — first England, then France, Germany and the United States — have exported large amounts of capital, and that the financial returns from these investments in many instances came to overshadow completely the income derived by the lending countries from foreign trade. It is also indisputable that industry embarked upon the road to concentration and monopoly, that increased efficiency in production led to larger profits and to the amassing of ever greater surpluses of capital. We must recognize further that, as a general rule, the return from investments abroad was distinctly above the return on reinvestment in home industry. In other words, the postulates of the socialist theory undoubtedly existed. There is no mentionable reason why the development of the capitalist system should not have had the results attributed to it.

But, as it happens, the actual course

[1] I strongly suspect that Hobson, in turn, took over the idea from the very bourgeois American financial expert, Charles A. Conant, whose remarkable article, "The Economic Basis of Imperialism," in the *North American Review*, September 1898, pp. 326–340, is now forgotten, but deserves recognition.

of history refutes the thesis. The course of British investment abroad shows that there was a very considerable export of capital before 1875, that is, during the climax of anti-imperialism in England. Between 1875 and 1895, while the tide of imperialism was coming to the full, there was a marked falling off of foreign investment. Capital export was then resumed on a large scale in the years before the war, though England was, in this period, already somewhat disillusioned by the outcome of the South African adventure and rather inclined to be skeptical about imperialism. Similar observations hold true of the United States. If the promulgation of the Monroe Doctrine was an act of imperialism, where was the export of capital which ought to have been its condition? Let us concede that the war with Spain was an imperialist episode. At that time the United States was still a debtor nation, importing rather than exporting capital. In Russia, too, the heyday of imperialism coincided with a period of heavy borrowing rather than of lending.

There is this further objection to be raised against the view of Hobson and his Neo-Marxian followers, that the export of capital seems to have little direct connection with territorial expansion. France, before the war, had plenty of capital to export, and some of her earliest and most vigorous imperialists, like Jules Ferry, declared that she required colonies in order to have adequate fields for the placement of this capital. But when France had secured colonies, she did not send her capital to them. By far the larger part of her exported funds went to Russia, Rumania, Spain and Portugal, Egypt and the Ottoman Empire. In 1902 only two or two and a half billion francs out of a total foreign investment of some 30 or 35 billion francs was placed in the colonies. In 1913 Britain had more money invested in the United States than in any colony or other foreign country. Less than half of her total export of capital had been to other parts of the Empire. The United States put more capital into the development of Canada than did England; and when, after the war, the United States became a great creditor nation, 43 percent of her investment was in Latin America, 27 percent in Canada and Newfoundland, and 22 percent in European countries. What she sent to her colonies was insignificant. Or let us take Germany, which in 1914 had about 25 billion marks placed abroad. Of this total only three percent was invested in Asia and Africa, and of that three percent only a small part in her colonies. Pre-war Russia was a great imperialist power, but Russia had to borrow from France the money invested in her Far Eastern projects. In our own day two of the most outspokenly imperialist powers, Japan and Italy, are both nations poor in capital. Whatever the urge that drives them to expansion, it cannot be the need for the export of capital.

At the height of the imperialist tide, let us say from 1885 to 1914, there was much less talk among the advocates of expansion about the need for foreign investment fields than about the need for new markets and for the safeguarding of markets from the tariff restrictions of competitors. It is certain that in the opinion of contemporaries that was the mainspring of the whole movement. But this economic explanation, like the other, has not been borne out by the actual developments. Very few colonies have done even half of their trading with the mother country and many have done less. Taken in the large it can be proved statistically that the colonial trade has always played a relatively unimportant part in the total foreign commerce of the great industrial nations. These nations have always been each other's best customers and no amount of rivalry and competition has prevented their trade from following, not the flag, but the price list. The position of Canada within the British Empire did not prevent her from levying tariffs against British goods, nor from developing exceedingly close economic relations with the United States. In the pre-war period German commerce with the British possessions was expanding at a relatively higher rate than was Britain's.

If one must have an economic interpretation of imperialism, one will probably find its historical evolution to have been something like this: In the days of England's industrial preëminence she was, by the very nature of the case, interested in free trade. In the palmiest days of Cobdenism she exported manufactured goods to the four corners of the earth, but she exported also machinery and other producers' goods, thereby preparing the way for the industrialization of the continental nations and latterly of other regions of the world. In order to protect their infant industries from British competition, these new industrial Powers threw over the teachings of the Manchester school and began to set up tariffs. The result was that the national markets were set aside, to a large extent, for home industry. British trade was driven to seek new markets, where the process was repeated. But the introduction of protective tariffs had this further effect, that it made possible the organization of cartels and trusts, that is, the concentration of industry, the increase of production and the lowering of costs. Surplus goods and low prices caused the other industrial Powers likewise to look abroad for additional markets, and, while this development was taking place, technological improvements were making transportation and communication safer and more expeditious. The exploration of Africa at that time was probably a pure coincidence, but it contributed to the movement toward trade and expansion and the growth of a world market. Fear that the newly opened areas of the world might be taken over by others and then enclosed in tariff walls led directly to the scramble for territory in Asia and Africa.

The socialist writers would have us believe that concentration in industry made for monopoly and that the banks, undergoing the same process of evolution, were, through their connection with industry, enabled to take over control of the whole capitalist system. They were the repositories of the surplus capital accumulated by a monopolistic system and they were therefore the prime movers in the drive for imperial expansion, their problem being to find fields for the investment of capital. This is an argument which does violence to the facts as they appear historically. The socialist writers almost to a man argue chiefly from the example of Germany, where cartellization came early and where the concentration of banking and the control of industry by the banks went further than in most countries. But even in Germany the movement towards overseas expansion came before the growth of monopoly and the amalgamation of the banks. In England, the imperialist country *par excellence*, there was no obvious connection between the two phenomena. The trust movement came late and never went as far as in Germany. The same was true of the consolidation of the banking system. One of the perennial complaints in England was the lack of proper coördination between the banks and industry. To a certain extent the English exported capital because the machinery for foreign investment was better than the organization for home investment. In the United States, to be sure,

there was already a pronounced concentration of industry when the great outburst of imperialism came in the last years of the past century, but in general the trust movement ran parallel to the movement for territorial expansion. In any event, it would be hard to disprove the contention that the growth of world trade and the world market brought on the tendency toward better organization and concentration in industry, rather than the reverse. It is obvious not only that one large unit can manufacture more cheaply than many small ones, but that it can act more efficiently in competition with others in the world market.

But this much is clear — that territorial control of extra-European territory solved neither the trade problem nor the question of surplus capital. The white colonies, which were the best customers, followed their own economic interests and not even tariff restrictions could prevent them from doing so. In the backward, colored, tropical colonies, which could be more easily controlled and exploited, it proved difficult to develop a market, because of the low purchasing power of the natives. The question of raw materials, of which so much has always been made, also remained open. The great industrial countries got but a fraction of their raw materials from the colonies, and the colonies themselves continued to show a tendency to sell their products in the best market. As for the export of capital, that continued to flow in an ever broader stream, not because the opportunities for investment at home were exhausted, but because the return from foreign investment was apt to be better and because, in many cases, foreign investment was the easier course. Capital flowed from the great industrial countries of Europe, but it did not flow to their colonies. The United States and Canada, Latin

America (especially the Argentine) and even old countries like Austria-Hungary and Russia, got the bulk of it. The export of capital necessarily took the form of the extension of credit, which in turn implied the transfer of goods. Not infrequently the granting of loans was made conditional on trade concessions by the borrowing country. So we come back to the question of trade and tariffs. In a sense the export of capital was nothing but a device to stimulate trade and to circumvent tariff barriers, which brings us back to the coincidence of the movement for protection and the movement toward imperialism.

This may seem like an oversimplified explanation and it probably is. Some may argue that imperialism is more than a movement toward territorial expansion and that financial imperialism in particular lays the iron hand of control on many countries supposedly independent. But if you try to divorce imperialism from territorial control you will get nowhere. Practically all writers on the subject have been driven to the conclusion that the problem cannot be handled at all unless you restrict it in this way. When Hobson wrote on imperialism, he had reference to the great spectacle of a few Powers taking over tremendous areas in Africa and Asia. Imperialism is, in a sense, synonymous with the appropriation by the western nations of the largest part of the rest of the world. If you take it to be anything else, you will soon be lost in nebulous concepts and bloodless abstractions. If imperialism is to mean any vague interference of traders and bankers in the affairs of other countries, you may as well extend it to cover any form of influence. You will have to admit cultural imperialism, religious imperialism, and what not. Personally I prefer to stick by a measurable, manageable concept.

But even though Hobson's idea, that imperialism "is the endeavor of the great controllers of industry to broaden the channel for the flow of their surplus wealth by seeking foreign markets and foreign investments to take off the goods and capital they cannot sell or use at home," proved to be the most stimulating and fertile of his arguments, he had the very correct idea that imperialism was also a "medley of aims and feelings." He had many other contributory explanations of the phenomenon. For example, he was keenly aware of the relationship between democracy and imperialism. The enfranchisement of the working classes and the introduction of free education had brought the rank and file of the population into the political arena. One result of this epoch-making change was the rise of the so-called yellow press, which catered to the common man's love of excitement and sensationalism. Northcliffe was one of the first to sense the value of imperialism as a "talking point." Colonial adventure and far-away conflict satisfied the craving for excitement of the industrial and white-collar classes which had to find some outlet for their "spectatorial lust." The upper crust of the working class, as Lenin admitted, was easily converted to the teaching of imperialism and took pride in the extension of empire.

No doubt this aspect of the problem is important. The mechanization of humanity in an industrial society is a phenomenon with which we have become all too familiar, and every thoughtful person now recognizes the tremendous dangers inherent in the powers which the demagogue can exercise through the press, the motion picture and the radio. In Hobson's day propaganda was still carried on primarily through the press, but later developments were already foreshadowed in the activities of a Northcliffe or a Hearst. Hobson himself was able to show how, during the war in South Africa, the English press took its information from the South African press, which had been brought very largely under the control of Rhodes and his associates. Even at that time Hobson and others were pointing out how imperialistic capital was influencing not only the press, but the pulpit and the universities. Indeed, Hobson went so far as to claim that the great inert mass of the population, who saw the tangled maze of world movements through dim and bewildered eyes, were the inevitable dupes of able, organized interests who could lure or scare or drive them into any convenient course.

Recognizing as we do that control of the public mind involves the most urgent political problems of the day, it is nevertheless important to point out that there is nothing inexorable about the connection of propaganda and imperialism. Even if you admit that a generation ago moneyed interests believed that imperialism was to their advantage, that these interests exercised a far-reaching control over public opinion, and that they used this control to dupe the common man into support of imperial ventures, it is obvious that at some other time these same interests might have different ideas with regard to their own welfare, just as it is evident that public opinion may be controlled by some other agency — the modern dictator, for example.

But the same thing is not true of another influence upon which Hobson laid great stress, namely the biological conception of politics and international relations. During the last years of the nineteenth century the ideas of "social Darwinism," as it was called, carried everything before them. Darwin's catchwords — the struggle for existence and the survival of the

fittest — which he himself always refused to apply to the social organism, were snapped up by others who were less scrupulous, and soon became an integral part of popular and even official thought on foreign affairs. It not only served to justify the ruthless treatment of the "backward" races and the carving up *in spe* of the Portuguese, Spanish, Ottoman and Chinese Empires and of other "dying nations," as Lord Salisbury called them, but it put the necessary imprimatur on the ideas of conflict between the great imperialistic Powers themselves, and supplied a divine sanction for expansion. It was currently believed, in the days of exuberant imperialism, that the world would soon be the preserve of the great states — the British, the American and the Russian — and it was deduced from this belief that survival in the struggle for existence was in itself adequate evidence of superiority and supernatural appointment. The British therefore looked upon their empire as a work of the divine will, while the Americans and Russians were filled with the idea of a manifest destiny. It will be at once apparent that glorification of war and joy in the conflict was intimately connected with the evolutionary mentality. Hobson, the most determined of anti-imperialists, was finally driven to define the whole movement as "a depraved choice of national life, imposed by self-seeking interests which appeal to the lusts of quantitative acquisitiveness and of forceful domination surviving in a nation from early centuries of animal struggle for existence."

The last phrases of this quotation will serve to lead us to the consideration of what has proved to be another fruitful thought of Hobson. He speaks, in one place, of imperialism as a sociological atavism, a remnant of the roving instinct, just as hunting and sport are left-overs of the physical struggle for existence. This idea of the roving instinct has made but little appeal to later writers, but the basic interpretation of imperialism as an atavism underlies the ingenious and highly intelligent essay of Joseph Schumpeter, "Zur Soziologie der Imperialism,"[2] the only work from the bourgeois side which has had anything like the influence exerted by the writers of the socialist school. Schumpeter, who is an eminent economist, worked out a most convincing argument to prove that imperialism has nothing to do with capitalism, and that it is certainly not a development of capitalism. Capitalism, he holds, is by nature opposed to expansion, war, armaments and professional militarism, and imperialism is nothing but an atavism, one of those elements of the social structure which cannot be explained from existing conditions, but only from the conditions of the past. It is, in other words, a hangover from a preceding economic order. Imperialism antedates capitalism, going back at least to the time of the Assyrians and Egyptians. It is, according to Schumpeter, the disposition of a state to forceful expansion without any special object and without a definable limit. Conquests are desired not so much because of their advantages, which are often questionable, but merely for the sake of conquest, success and activity.

Schumpeter's theory is in some ways extravagant, but it has served as the starting point for some very interesting speculation, especially among German scholars of the liberal persuasion. It is now fairly clear, I think, that the Neo-Marxian critics have paid far too little attention to the imponderable, psychological ingredients of imperialism. The movement may, with-

out much exaggeration, be interpreted not only as an atavism, as a remnant of the days of absolute monarchy and mercantilism, when it was to the interest of the prince to increase his territory and the number of his subjects, but also as an aberration, to be classed with the extravagances of nationalism. Just as nationalism can drive individuals to the point of sacrificing their very lives for the purposes of the state, so imperialism has driven them to the utmost exertions and the extreme sacrifice, even though the stake might be only some little known and at bottom valueless part of Africa or Asia. In the days when communication and economic interdependence have made the world one in so many ways, men still interpret international relations in terms of the old cabinet policies, they are still swayed by out-moded, feudalistic ideas of honor and prestige.

In a sense, then, you can say that there is, in every people, a certain indefinable national energy, which may find expression in a variety of ways.

As a general rule great domestic crises and outbursts of expansion follow each other in the history of the world. In many of the continental countries of Europe, and for that matter in our own country, great internal problems were fought out in the period before 1870. The energies which, in Germany and Italy, went into the victory of the national cause, soon began to project themselves beyond the frontiers. While the continental nations were settling great issues between them, England sat "like a bloated Quaker, rubbing his hands at the roaring trade" he was carrying on. In those days the British cared very little for their empire. Many of them would have felt relieved if the colonies had broken away without a fuss. But, says Egerton, the best-known historian of British colonial policy, when the

[2] "Zur Soziologie der Imperialism," by Josef Schumpeter. Tübingen: Mohr, 1919, 76 p.

Germans and the French began to show an interest in colonial expansion, then the British began to think that there must be some value as yet undiscovered in the colonies. They not only started a movement to bind the colonies and the mother country more closely together, but they stretched out their hands for more. In the end they, who had the largest empire to begin with, got easily the lion's share of the yet unappropriated parts of the world. Some thought they were engaged in the fulfilment of a divine mission to abolish slavery, to spread the gospel, to clothe and educate the heathen. Others thought they were protecting the new markets from dangerous competitors, securing their supply of raw materials, or finding new fields for investment. But underlying the whole imperial outlook there was certainly more than a little misapprehension of economics, much self-delusion and self-righteousness, much misapplication of evolutionary teaching and above all much of the hoary tradition of honor, prestige, power and even plain combativeness. Imperialism always carries with it the connotation of the *Imperator* and of the tradition of rule. It is bound up with conscious or subconscious ideas of force, of brutality, of ruthlessness. It was these traits and tendencies that were so vividly expressed in the poetry and stories of Kipling, and it was his almost uncanny ability to sense the emotions of his time and people that made him the greatest apostle of imperialism.

We shall not go far wrong, then, if we stress the psychological and political factors in imperialism as well as its economic and intellectual elements. It was, of course, connected closely with the great changes in the social structure of the western world, but it was also a projection of nationalism beyond the boundaries of Europe, a projection on a world scale of the time-honored struggle for power and for a balance of power as it had existed on the Continent for centuries. The most casual perusal of the literature of imperialism will reveal the continued potency of these atavistic motives. . . .

We need not pursue this subject in all its minute details. The point I want to make is that in the case of Japan, as in the case of many other countries, it is easier to show that the military and official classes are a driving force behind the movement for expansion than to show that a clique of nefarious bankers or industrialists is the determining factor. Business interests may have an interest in the acquisition of territory, or they may not. But military and official classes almost always have. War is, for the soldiers, a profession, and it is no mere chance that war and imperialism are so commonly lumped together. For officials, expansion means new territories to govern and new jobs to be filled. . . .

Charles A. Beard: TERRITORIAL EXPANSION CONNECTED WITH COMMERCE

WITHIN a few years the movement for territorial expansion, conforming to the commercial type, was renewed in the Caribbean direction, with the Cuban revolution of 1895 as the occasion for action. Great and genuine as was the indignation throughout the United States at the horrors in Cuba which marked the contest between Spain and the revolutionists, it was accompanied by other considerations belonging under the head of national interest. There were many practical reasons for American intervention. The passion for annexation that sprang from the desire to extend the slave power to Cuba had, of course, disappeared with the abolition of slavery; but other grounds for anxiety over the fate of the Island remained. Fundamental among them were incentives connected with national defense, formulated under the aegis of the Monroe Doctrine. Entirely apart from the antagonism between the monarchical institutions of the Old World and the republican institutions of the New, which figured so conspicuously in the original Doctrine, the United States could not fail to regard the establishment of a first-rate military or naval power in Cuba as a menace to its security, involving huge outlays for defensive purpose and the constant peril of a serious war. Nor did the Government of the United States look upon the permanent possession of the Island by Spain as conducive to the most efficient development of insular economy and trade.

Supplementary interests were plainly economic. The cane sugar growers of Louisiana could supply only a small part of the domestic requirement and the beet-sugar industry was in its infancy. Under reciprocity arrangements with Spain sugar had been allowed to come freely into the United States from Cuba for many years; in 1898 ninety-five percent of Cuba's export to the United States was sugar and that amounted to a significant proportion of Cuba's foreign trade. During the rapid development of the Cuban sugar industry, which responded to the enormous demand of the American market, American capital and enterprise poured into Cuban plantations and mills. Then came the tariff of 1894 which put a duty on raw and refined sugars. This was followed by a heavy drop in the export of sugar from Cuba to the United States, widespread unemployment and distress in Cuba, revolutionary outbreaks, and the destruction of American property as well as American business with the Island.

In his message of December 7, 1896, President Cleveland explained how the Cuban revolution spread economic ruin throughout Cuba. After describing the methods pursued by bands of marauders which now in the name of one party and then of another, plundered the people and harried the country, the President said: "Such a condition of things would inevitably entail immense destruction of property, even if it were the policy of both parties to prevent it as far as practicable; but while such seemed to be the original policy of the Spanish government, it has now apparently abandoned it and is acting upon the same theory as the insurgents, namely, that the exigencies of the contest require the wholesale annihilation of property that it may not be of use and advantage to the enemy. It is to the same end that, in pursuance of general orders, Spanish garrisons are now being withdrawn from plantations and the rural population required to concentrate itself in the towns. The sure result would seem to be that the industrial value of the Island is fast diminishing and that unless there is a speedy and radical change in existing conditions it will soon disappear altogether."

While making due allowance for the sympathy of the American people for the suffering Cubans and for the efforts of the revolutionists to establish "better and freer government," President Cleveland pointed out that the United States had a concern with the situation "which is by no means of a wholly sentimental or philanthropic character. It lies so near to us as to be hardly separated from our territory. Our actual pecuniary interest in it is second only to that of the people and government of Spain. It is reasonably estimated that at least from $30,000,000 to $50,000,000 of American capital are invested in the plantations and in railroad, mining, and other business enterprises on the Island. The volume of trade between the United States and Cuba, which in 1889 amounted to about $64,000,000, rose in 1893 to about $103,000,000 and in 1894, the year before the present insurrection broke out, amounted to nearly $96,000,000."

Although it was the custom of the Spanish government to represent the revolution as the work of "the scum" of the Island, that view was one-sided, to say the least. Secretary Olney insisted that "the Cuban insurgents are not to be regarded as the scum of the earth. . . . In sympathy and feeling nine-tenths of the Cuban population are with them. . . . The property class to a man is disgusted with Spanish misrule, with a system which has burdened the Island with $300,000,000 of debt, whose impositions in the way of annual taxes just stop short of prohibiting all industrial enterprise, and which yet does not fulfil the primary functions of government by insuring safety to life and security to property." In other words, substantial native interests in Cuba were on the side of American economic interests in the Island during the movement to throw off Spanish rule and stabilize the social order.

Yet President Cleveland, as leader of Jefferson's old agrarian party, then harassed by extreme agrarians known as Populists, was not prepared to wage war on Spain or forcibly intervene in behalf of Cuban independence. The initiative was left to the Republicans who, as heirs of the Whig and Federalist tradition, could interpret national interest in terms of commercial expansion and the enlargement of naval power. In their platform of 1896 the Republicans stated their case succinctly without any embroidery of political theory: "The government of Spain, having lost control of Cuba, and being unable to protect the property or lives of resident American citizens, or to comply with its treaty obligations, we believe that the Government of the United States should actively use its influence and good offices to restore peace and give independence to the Island." This declaration, with its inevitable implications, was accompanied by an appropriate navy plank: "The peace and security of the republic and the maintenance of its rightful influence among the nations of the earth demand a naval power commensurate with its position and responsibility. We therefore favor the continued enlargement of the navy and a complete system of harbor and coast defenses."

If, as seems highly probable in view of the documents now available, the independence of Cuba could have been obtained by diplomatic pressure on Spain, the administration of President McKinley did not choose that course. The mere emancipation of Cuba from Spanish dominion would not have given the United States a naval base at Guantanamo, commanding the Windward passage; nor would it have furnished the occasion for annexing Porto Rico, commanding the Mona passage, or for acquiring the Philippines which supplied a naval base for commercial expansion in the Orient, so long and so ardently demanded by American naval officers.

To be sure, no such comprehensive policy of expansion, if deliberately formulated by the American Government, was proclaimed officially to the country as a motive for war. In the face of the Teller amendment to the resolution declaring war on Spain, which disowned motives of annexation and renounced any intention to impose restraints on the independence of Cuba, it would have been inexpedient to publish any such program, had it been privately entertained. Indeed the war sentiment stirred up in the United States scarcely ran beyond assistance to "the heroic Cubans" struggling for independence, as the American colonists had done more than a hundred years before, and the letters and papers of the time now open to students reveal no little confusion in official minds.

Yet the conformity of the outcome to the pattern of commercial and naval expansion could not have been neater, had

it been deliberately planned. Nor could it be accurately described as a historic accident, as was once the fashion; for it was the perfect upshot of a long chain of actions and leadership extending back over more than half a century. Daniel Webster, Commodore Perry, William H. Seward, and Admiral Meade had not wrought in vain. While many congressmen who voted for war did not look far ahead, Theodore Roosevelt, Henry Cabot Lodge, and Alfred Thayer Mahan saw beyond the smoke of battle — how far and with what vision the verdict of history remains unspoken.

Without in the slightest minimizing the lofty sentiments which accompanied the war of the United States on Spain, it remains a fact that the American interests associated with Cuban industry and trade derived practical benefits from forcible intervention and expanded under the rule of law later established in virtue of the Platt Amendment. After the war was over American claims for damages done during the revolution were adjusted on an equitable basis and industry and commerce flourished as never under the Spanish régime. The American capital invested in Cuba, estimated by President Cleveland at a figure ranging between $30,000,000 and $50,000,000 in 1896, rose to $141,000,000 within ten years after the conclusion of peace. At the beginning of 1931 the total investment of American capital was placed at $1,066,551,000, consisting of $935,706,000 in "direct" investments, such as sugar properties and enterprises, electric utilities, transportation and communication systems, and other tangible properties; and of $130,845,000 in "portfolio" investments comprising a broad range of securities. The volume of trade, which President Cleveland put at $96,000,000 in 1895, increased rapidly as soon as stability was assured in the Island,

and within less than thirty years stood at $561,499,000 — $199,778,000 in exports from the United States to Cuba and $361,-721,000 in imports from Cuba into the United States. . . .

Although great emphasis was laid by the Government of the United States on the weight of "moral obligation" in shaping its decision to acquire the Philippine Islands at the close of the Spanish war, this obligation was not the sole consideration. Practical interests also entered into the calculations, more or less, from the beginning of the conflict. American trade in the Orient had been an object of solicitude on the part of the Government from the foundation of the Republic. It was included by the authors of the *Federalist* in the list of commercial interests abroad deserving support by the political agencies to be established under the Constitution. And during the long period that intervened between the inauguration of Washington and the inauguration of McKinley, Presidents, Secretaries of State, Secretaries of the Navy, and innumerable naval officers gave serious attention to the promotion of American commercial interests in the Far East. The promotion of commerce involved the securing of territorial footholds to serve as bases for the navy and as points of support for demonstrations of naval power against rivals and disturbers of the order necessary for regular traffic in goods. The logic, once the premises were accepted, appeared irresistible. As expounded by Mahan the fundamental truth was that the control of the seas, especially along the great lines drawn by national interest, is the chief among the material elements in the power and prosperity of nations; and "From this necessarily follows the principle that, as subsidiary to such control, it is imperative to take possession, when it can righteously be done, of such mari-

time positions as contribute to secure command." A review of these commercial activities, extensions of naval power, efforts to get naval stations, and declarations of policy on the part of the American Government and American naval officers shows that there was nothing new in the motives which actuated the McKinley administration in the conquest and acquisition of the Philippines.

Whatever may have been the divided state of President McKinley's mind during and immediately after the Spanish war, it is certain that ardent members of his party, particularly Senator Henry Cabot Lodge and Theodore Roosevelt, Assistant Secretary of the Navy at the outbreak of the war, had clearly in view the possibility of securing a permanent base in the Philippines for the extension of American power in the Orient. In a letter written to Mr. Lodge on September 21, 1897, six months before the declaration of war, Mr. Roosevelt stated that he had recently dined with President McKinley and had expounded his opinions to the President on action to be taken in case a war broke out with Spain. "I gave him a paper showing exactly where all our ships are, and I also sketched in outline what I thought ought to be done if things looked menacing about Spain, urging the necessity of taking an immediate and prompt initiative if we wished to avoid the chance of some serious trouble, and of the Japs chipping in." After sketching the lines of action along the Cuban coast, Mr. Roosevelt added, "Meanwhile, our Asiatic squadron should blockade, and if possible, take Manila."

Resolved to have a man in charge of the Asiatic squadron, "who would act without referring things back to home authorities," Mr. Roosevelt, as Assistant Secretary of the Navy, selected Commodore Dewey. He advised Dewey to ask

Senator Proctor for support, and the Senator acted promptly by calling on President McKinley and getting a promise of the appointment before he left the White House. After receiving his commission, Dewey sailed for his post on December 7, 1898, and set to work to assemble the fleet at Hong Kong, as he said himself, "entirely on my own initiative, without any hint whatever from the department that hostilities might be expected. It was evident that in case of emergency Hong Kong was the most advantageous position from which to move to the attack." A little more than two months later, Assistant Secretary Roosevelt sent Dewey an order to gather the squadron, except the *Monocacy*, at Hong Kong, to "keep full of coal, and in event of war to see that the Spanish squadron does not leave the Asiatic coast, and then resort to offensive operations in the Philippine Islands." After the declaration of war, Secretary Long instructed Dewey to proceed at once to the Philippine Islands and use utmost endeavor. "Thus," claims Mr. Roosevelt's biographer, "was the famous battle of Manila fought and won by a commander whose appointment had been secured by Roosevelt against the wishes of Secretary Long and whose fleet had been thoroughly equipped for the conflict by an order that Roosevelt had sent on his own responsibility in the absence of his chief."

On May 24, 1898, about a month after the opening of the war, Mr. Lodge wrote to Colonel Roosevelt, then with his regiment: "The one point where haste is needed is the Philippines, and I think I can say to you, in confidence but in absolute certainty, that the Administration is grasping the whole policy at last. . . . Porto Rico is not forgotten and we mean to have it. Unless I am utterly and profoundly mistaken, the Administration is now fully committed to the large policy we both desire." The next day Colonel Roosevelt wrote to Mr. Lodge: "I earnestly hope that no truce will be granted and that peace will only be made on consideration of Cuba being independent, Porto Rico ours, and the Philippines taken away from Spain." A month later Mr. Lodge was able to write Colonel Roosevelt, forecasting precisely the ultimate action taken by President McKinley. He stated that he had recently dined with Mr. Day, Secretary of State, and Captain Mahan, the distinguished American formulator of *Machtpolitik*, and that he had "talked the Philippines" with Mr. Day for two hours. "He said at the end," continued Mr. Lodge, "that he thought we could not escape our destiny there. The feeling of the country is overwhelming against giving the Philippines back to Spain. That is clear to the most casual observer. Bryan has announced that he is against colonization, and Cleveland, in a ponderous speech, has come out against war as much as he dares and utterly against annexation. We shall sweep the country on that issue in my judgment."

Thus, in spite of numerous references to fate, the accidents of history, the current of events, destiny, and gifts of the gods, it is clear that there was a positive connection between the decision to annex the Philippine Islands and the official activities of the Government of the United States in the Far East, extending over a century of commercial development, accompanied by avowed resolutions of naval officers with respect to naval bases and points of naval support for trade. Other evidence confirms this view. President McKinley, as Senator Hoar said, "had to get his facts" about the Philippines, "almost wholly" from military and naval officers during the summer of 1898; and numerous military and naval officers were dispatched to Paris for the purpose of giving the American Peace Commission their views on the policy to be pursued with respect to the Philippines. While the sincerity of President McKinley's personal misgivings is evident in the records, it cannot be denied that powerful groups in the official world and outside regarded the annexation of the Philippines as a desirable consummation of ardent labors extending over a long period of history. The chain of connections is too close and too strong to be broken by emphasis on the uncertainties and hesitancy prevalent in many circles during the summer of 1898.

Nor did President McKinley himself, while laying stress on the element of moral obligation, overlook the force of practical interest connected with the historical development of American commerce in the Orient. Although the peace protocol left the issue of the Philippines open and President McKinley informed the mediator, M. Jules Cambon, that the peace negotiators were to determine it, he ordered the American commissioners, in his opening instructions to them, to demand the cession of the Island of Luzon in full right and sovereignty and equal favors for American ships and merchandise in the ports left to Spain. In support of this demand, the President said, "Inci-

dental to our tenure in the Philippines is the commercial opportunity to which American statesmanship cannot be indifferent. It is just to use every legitimate means for the enlargement of American trade; but we seek no advantages in the Orient which are not common to all. Asking only the open door for ourselves, we are ready to accord the open door to others. The commercial opportunity which is naturally and inevitably associated with this new opening depends less on large territorial possessions than upon an adequate commercial basis and upon broad and equal privileges." Yet, Tyler Dennett remarks, "a fortuitous concurrence of events had brought within American grasp the very expedient which Commodore Perry and Dr. Peter Parker had urged in 1853 and 1857. Manila might become the equivalent for Hong Kong and the leased ports of China, for the lack of which American trade and interests in the Far East were, in the summer of 1898, in serious prospective if not present embarrassment." A long series of commercial and naval efforts, deliberately conceived in terms of interest and far from accidental in character, had produced a desired result. No apparently fortuitous aspects could obscure the long-sustained purpose which had at last borne fruit. . . .

Julius W. Pratt: AMERICAN BUSINESS AND THE SPANISH–AMERICAN WAR

THE student who seeks from the standard historians an explanation of why the United States embarked upon the war with Spain and the resulting

career of territorial expansion and imperialism can hardly fail to meet with two contradictory opinions. James Ford Rhodes, whose close relations with Mark

From Julius W. Pratt, "American Business and the Spanish-American War," *Hispanic American Historical Review*, XIV (May, 1934), 163–201. Used by permission. NOTE: For footnotes see the original. Ed.

Hanna enabled him to speak with much authority of the attitude of American business men, has stated in no uncertain terms that "the financial and business interests of the country were opposed to the war." According to this thesis, the war resulted from a combination of humanitarian sympathy for Cuba and popular excitement skillfully engineered by the sensational press, and the annexations which followed were accepted as unsought responsibilities thrust upon the nation by the exigencies of the war. On the other hand, Professor H. U. Faulkner, in his excellent *American Economic History*, contends that the expansion of American industrial and financial power had created a readiness for "financial imperialism," which "provided the great cause for the war." These two opinions seem irreconcilable. How could the war be caused primarily by the desire of American industry and finance for imperial expansion, and at the same time be opposed by "the financial and business interests of the country"?

Two separate but related questions here call for examination. First, can we accept Rhodes's generalization that American business was opposed to a course which would lead to war with Spain? Second, did American business and finance display an interest in acquiring colonies either before war was declared or in the months between the declaration and the peace treaty? Evidence bearing upon these two questions has been sought in a large number of financial and trade periodicals which supposedly spoke the minds of their clientele, in proceedings of chambers of commerce and boards of trade, and in the *Miscellaneous Files* in the department of state, containing letters and petitions from business men and organizations. While conclusions drawn from such data are subject to the dangers which beset all studies of public opinion, there seems, on each question, a sufficient preponderance of evidence to warrant a fairly confident answer.

That business sentiment, especially in the east, was strongly anti-war at the close of 1897 and in the opening months of 1898, is hardly open to doubt. Wall Street stocks turned downward whenever the day's news seemed to presage war and climbed again with information favorable to peace. Bulls and bears on the market were those who anticipated, respectively, a peaceable and a warlike solution of the Cuban question. The "jingo," in congress or the press, was an object of intense dislike to the editors of business and financial journals, who sought to counteract his influence by anti-war editorials in their columns. Boards of trade and chambers of commerce added their pleas for the maintenance of peace to those of the business newspapers and magazines. So marked, indeed, was the anti-war solidarity of the financial interests and their spokesmen that the jingoes fell to charging Wall Street with want of patriotism. Wall Street, declared the Sacramento *Evening Bee* (March 11, 1898), was "the colossal and aggregate Benedict Arnold of the Union, and the syndicated Judas Iscariot of humanity." Senator Thurston, of Nebraska, charged that opposition to war was found only among the "money-changers," bringing from the editor of *The American Banker* the reply that "there is not an intelligent, self-respecting and civilized American citizen anywhere who would not prefer to have the existing crisis culminate in peaceful negotiations."

This anti-war attitude on the part of several leading financial journals continued up to the very beginning of hostilities. The New York *Journal of Commerce and Commercial Bulletin* declared on February 28 that the only possible excuses for war would be (1) a finding by the naval board investigating the *Maine* disaster that the ship had been destroyed by an official act of the Spanish Government; or (2) a refusal by Spain to make reparation if the board should hold that that country had failed to exercise due diligence in safeguarding the vessel. Either of these events it held to be almost inconceivable. The *Commercial and Financial Chronicle* expressed the belief on March 12 that the opposition of the financial interests would yet prevent war; and on April 2 the same journal branded as "monstrous" the proposition to settle the Cuban and *Maine* questions by war while the slightest chance remained for a peaceful solution. And on April 16, after the House of Representatives had passed the Cuban resolutions, the Boston *Journal of Commerce* declared: "Sober second thought had but little to do with the deliberations. . . . The members were carried off their feet by the war fever that had been so persistently worked up since the *Maine* explosion. . . ."

The reasons for this attitude on the part of business are not far to seek. Since the panic of 1893 American business had been in the doldrums. Tendencies toward industrial revival had been checked, first by the Venezuela war scare in December, 1895, and again by the free silver menace in 1896. But in 1897 began a real revival, and before the end of the year signs of prosperity appeared on all sides. The *New York Commercial* conducted a survey of business conditions in a wide variety of trades and industries, from which it concluded that, "After three years of waiting and of false starts, the groundswell of demand has at last begun to rise with a steadiness which leaves little doubt that an era of prosperity has appeared." January, 1898, said the same article, is "a supreme moment in the period of transition

from depression to comparative prosperity." This note of optimism one meets at every turn, even in such a careful and conservative sheet as the *Commercial and Financial Chronicle*. As early as July, 1897, this paper remarked: "We appear to be on the eve of a revival in business"; and in December, after remarking upon the healthy condition of the railroads and the iron industry, it concluded: "In brief, no one can study the industrial condition of today in America without a feeling of elation. . . ." The *Wall Street Journal* found only two "blue spots" in the entire country: Boston, which suffered from the depressed demand for cotton goods, and New York, where senseless rate cutting by certain railroads caused uneasiness. "Throughout the west, southwest and on the Pacific Coast business has never been better, nor the people more hopeful." A potent cause for optimism was found in the striking expansion of the American export trade. A volume of exports far in excess of those of any recent year, a favorable balance of trade of $286,000,000, and an especially notable increase in exports of manufactures of iron, steel, and copper, convinced practically every business expert that the United States was on the point of capturing the markets of the world. "There is no question," said one journal, "that the world, generally, is looking more and more to the United States as the source of its supply for very many of the staple commodities of life." Especially elated were spokesmen of the iron and steel industry. Cheaper materials and improved methods were enabling the American producer to undersell his British competitor in Europe and in the British possessions, and Andrew Carnegie was talking of a great shipbuilding yard near New York to take advantage of these low costs. The *Iron Age,* in an editorial on "The Future of Business," foretold the abolition of the business cycle by means of a better planned economy, consolidation of railroads and industries, reductions of margins of profit, higher wages and lower prices to consumers — in other words a "new deal" resembling that attempted in 1933.

To this fair prospect of a great business revival the threat of war was like a specter at the feast. A foreign complication, thought the *Commercial and Financial Chronicle,* in October, 1897, would quickly mar "the trade prosperity which all are enjoying." Six months later (April 2, 1898), after a discussion of the effect of war rumors on the stock exchange, it declared: ". . . every influence has been, and even now is, tending strongly towards a term of decided prosperity, and that the Cuban disturbance, and it alone, has arrested the movement and checked enterprise." The *Banker and Tradesman* saw in the Cuban complication the threat of "a material setback to the prosperous conditions which had just set in after five years of panic and depression." The same journal summarized a calculation made by the Boston *Transcript* showing that in February, 1898, the wave of prosperity had carried the average price of twenty-five leading stocks to within 5½ points of the high for the preceding ten years and 30 points above the low of 1896, and that the Cuban trouble had, in a little over two months, caused a loss of over ten points, or more than one-third of the recent gain. "War would impede the march of prosperity and put the country back many years," said the *New Jersey Trade Review.* The *Railway Age* was of the opinion that the country was coming out of a depression and needed peace to complete its recovery. "From a commercial and mercenary standpoint," it remarked, "it seems peculiarly bitter that this war should have come when the

country had already suffered so much and so needed rest and peace."

The idea that war could bring any substantial benefits to business was generally scouted. It would endanger our currency stability, interrupt our trade, and threaten our coasts and our commerce, thought the *Commercial and Financial Chronicle.* It would "incalculably increase the loss to business interests," said the *Banker's Magazine:* while the *United States Investor* held that war was "never beneficial from a material standpoint, that is, in the long run." The *Railroad Gazette* predicted that war would result in "interruption of business enterprise of every kind, stopping new projects and diminution of the output of existing businesses and contraction of trade everywhere." Railroads would lose more than they would gain. Even arms manufacturers were not all agreed that war would be profitable. Journals speaking for the iron and steel industry also argued that war would injure business. It "would injure the iron and steel makers ten times as much as they would be benefited by the prevailing spurt in the manufacture of small arms, projectiles and steel plates for war ships," in the opinion of one of these. The *American Wool and Cotton Reporter* of New York and the *Northwestern Miller* of Minneapolis agreed that war was never materially beneficial in the long run, while trade journals in Atlanta, Chattanooga, and Portland, Oregon, saw as fruit of the approaching conflict only destruction, debt, and depressed industry.

Many conservative interests feared war for the specific reason that it might derange the currency and even revive the free-silver agitation, which had seemed happily dead. The subsidence of that agitation and the prospect of currency reform were among the hopeful factors at the close of 1897. It had been not uncommonly charged that the "jingoes" were animated in part by the expectation that war would lead to inflation in paper or silver. The New York *Journal of Commerce,* in an editorial on "The Breeding Grounds of Jingoism," had called attention to the fact that the jingoes were generally silverites, including in their number "the financiers who desire to force bankruptcy on the country as a means of breaking down the gold standard" and had quoted with approval an editorial from another paper charging that Senator Morgan's championship of the Cuban insurgents was part of "his wild scheming in the interest of the silver standard." The *Commercial and Financial Chronicle* endorsed this view, declaring that many of the Cuban agitators "are only interested in the establishment of a free-silver standard, a plan which they think war would advance." Similar views were expressed by the *American Banker* of New York, the *United States Investor* of Boston, and the *Rand-McNally Bankers' Monthly* of Chicago. The last-named quoted from a speech of Secretary of the Treasury Gage, delivered in Chicago in February, 1898, in which he had declared that "it would be scarcely possible for this nation to engage in war in its present condition . . . without a suspension of specie payments and a resort to further issues of Government notes." A war of any duration, in the opinion of the *United States Investor,* would certainly derange the currency and reduce business to a gambling basis.

Something of a freak among New York financial journals was the *Financial Record,* which, in November, 1897, denounced "the cowardice of our Administration in refusing the phenomenally brave Cubans the commonest rights of belligerency" as "a disgrace to the United States," and argued that war with Spain, far from depressing securities or injuring

business, "would vastly increase the net earning power of every security sold on our market today." The mystery of this jingo attitude is explained when we discover that this journal had been a warm advocate of the free coinage of silver, thus becoming clearly the exception that proves the rule.

Business opinion in the west, especially in the Mississippi Valley, appears to have been less opposed to war and less apprehensive of its results than that of the Atlantic coast. The Kansas City Board of Trade, at the beginning of 1897, had urged recognition of Cuban independence. The Cincinnati Chamber of Commerce, at a meeting on March 29, 1898, adopted "amidst much enthusiasm" resolutions condemning Spain for cruelties to the Cubans and the destruction of the *Maine* and calling for a "firm and vigorous policy which will have for its purpose — peacefully if we can, but with force if we must — the redress of past wrongs, and the complete and unqualified independence of Cuba." The Chicago *Economist* denied that war would seriously hurt business or endanger the gold standard and asserted that the liberation of Cuba, by peace or war, would mean another star of glory for the United States and would produce "results of the highest value to mankind." *The Rand-McNally Bankers' Monthly,* of the same city, while opposing war, called attention to the fact that while the war scare had demoralized the stock market, "general business activity apparently received an impetus." Similarly the *Age of Steel* (St. Louis), while much preferring peace "when not secured at the price of national honor," comforted its readers with the thought that although foreign trade might suffer, home trade and industries would be stimulated by war. A St. Louis bank president, Mr. Lackland, believed that war would "cause a boom in many lines of business in this country . . . and give employment to a large number of persons who are now out of work." The Chattanooga *Tradesman* stated on March 1, 1898, that a "small prospect" of war had already stimulated the iron trade in certain lines and had benefited the railroads by hurrying forward shipments of grain and other commodities in anticipation of war prices. The *Mining and Scientific Press,* of San Francisco, while holding that, in general, war "lets loose havoc and waste, and entails destructive expense," conceded that "to nearly everything related to the mining industry the war will be a stimulus."

Even in New York, business men saw some rays of light piercing the war clouds. Stock market operators, according to the *Wall Street Journal,* just after the *Maine* explosion, "did not look for any great break in the market, because actual war with Spain would be a very small affair compared with the Venezuela complication with Great Britain." Their expectation was for a drop in stocks at the beginning of hostilities, followed by a resumption of the recent advance. In fact, the first shock might well be followed by a boom. "The nation looks for peace," declared *Dun's Review,* March 5, "but knows that its sources of prosperity are quite beyond the reach of any attack that is possible." *Bradstreet's* contrasted the jumpiness of Wall Street over war news with "the calm way in which general business interests have regarded the current foreign complications"; and *Dun's Review* of March 12 stated that no industry or branch of business showed any restriction, while some had been rapidly gaining, that railroads were increasing their profits while speculators sold their stocks, and that there was a growing demand for the products of all the great industries.

Despite such expressions as these, there seems little reason to question the belief that an overwhelming preponderance of the vocal business interests of the country strongly desired peace. By the middle of March, however, many organs of business opinion were admitting that a war with Spain might bring no serious disaster, and there was a growing conviction that such a war was inevitable. In the senate on March 17, Senator Redfield Proctor of Vermont described, from his own observation, the terrible sufferings of the Cuban "reconcentrados." Proctor was no sensationalist, and his speech carried great weight. The *Wall Street Journal* described its effect among the denizens of the Street. "Senator Proctor's speech," it said, "converted a great many people in Wall Street, who have heretofore taken the ground that the United States had no business to interfere in a revolution on Spanish soil. These men had been among the most prominent in deploring the whole Cuban matter, but there was no question about the accuracy of Senator Proctor's statements and, as many of them expressed it, they made the blood boil." The *American Banker,* hitherto a firm opponent of intervention, remarked on March 23 that Proctor's speech showed an intolerable state of things, in view of which it could not understand "how any one with a grain of human sympathy within him can dispute the propriety of a policy of intervention, so only that this outraged people might be set free!" It still hoped, however, for a peaceful solution, declaring that the United States ought to urge the Cubans to accept the Spanish offer of autonomy. That this growing conviction that something must be done about Cuba was by no means equivalent to a desire for war, was clearly revealed a few days later. Rumors circulated to the effect that Spain was willing to sell Cuba and that J. P. Morgan's return from a trip abroad was connected with plans to finance the purchase. "There is much satisfaction expressed in Wall Street," said the *Wall Street Journal,* "at the prospects of having Cuba free, because it is believed that this will take one of the most disturbing factors out of the situation. . . . Even if $200,000,000 is the indemnity demanded it is a sum which the United States could well afford to pay to get rid of the trouble." Even $250,000,000, it was thought, would be insignificant in comparison with the probable cost of a war.

It remains to examine the attitude of certain American business men and corporations having an immediate stake in Cuba, or otherwise liable to be directly affected by American intervention. Much American capital, as is well known, was invested in the Cuban sugar industry. Upon this industry the civil war fell with peculiarly devastating effect, not only cutting off profits on capital so invested, but also crippling a valuable carrying trade between Cuba and the United States. Naturally enough, some firms suffering under these conditions desired to see the United States intervene to end the war, though such intervention might lead to war between the United States and Spain. In May, 1897, a memorial on the subject bearing over three hundred signatures was presented to John Sherman, Secretary of State. The signers described themselves as "citizens of the United States, doing business as bankers, merchants, manufacturers, steamship owners, and agents in the cities of Boston, New York, Philadelphia, Baltimore, Savannah, Charleston, Jacksonville, New Orleans, and other places, and also other citizens of the United States, who have been for many years engaged in the export and import trade with the Island of Cuba." They called attention to the serious losses to which their businesses had been sub-

jected by the hostilities in Cuba and expressed the hope that in order to prevent further loss, to reëstablish American commerce, and also to secure "the blessings of peace for one and a half millions of residents of the Island of Cuba now enduring unspeakable distress and suffering," the United States Government might take steps to bring about an honorable reconciliation between the parties to the conflict.

Another memorial, signed by many of the same subscribers, was presented to President McKinley on February 9, 1898, by a committee of New York business men. It asserted that the Cuban war, which had now continued for three entire years, had caused an average loss of $100,000,000 a year, or a total loss of $300,000,000 in the import and export trade between Cuba and the United States, to which were to be added

heavy sums irretrievably lost by the destruction of American properties, or properties supported by American capital in the Island itself, such as sugar factories, railways, tobacco plantations, mines and other industrial enterprises; the loss of the United States in trade and capital by means of this war being probably far greater and more serious than that of all the other parties concerned, not excepting Spain herself.

The sugar crop of 1897–1898, continued the memorial, appeared for the most part lost like its two predecessors, and unless peace could be established before May or June of the current year, the crop of 1898–1899, with all the business dependent upon it, would likewise be lost, since the rainy season of summer and fall would be required "to prepare for next winter's crop, by repairing damaged fields, machinery, lines of railways, &c." In view of the importance to the United States of the Cuban trade and of American participation "in the ownership or management of Cuban sugar factories, railways and other enterprises," the petitioners hoped that the president would deem the situation "of sufficient importance as to warrant prompt and efficient measures by our Government, with the sole object of restoring peace . . . and with it restoring to us a most valuable commercial field."

How much weight such pressure from special interests had with the administration there is no way of knowing. But it is to be noted that the pressure from parties directly interested was not all on one side. Mr. E. F. Atkins, an American citizen who divided his time between Boston and his sugar plantation of Soledad near Cienfuegos, Cuba, which he had developed at a cost of $1,400,000, had been able, through protection received from the Spanish Government and through a corps of guards organized and paid by himself, to continue operations throughout the period of the insurrection. He was frequently in Washington, where he had influential friends, during both the Cleveland and McKinley administrations and worked consistently against the adoption of any measures likely to provoke war. Unlike some of the sugar plantations, American-owned iron mines in Cuba continued to do active business despite the insurrection. Three American iron and manganese enterprises in the single province of Santiago claimed to have an investment of some $6,000,000 of purely American capital, a large proportion of which was in property which could easily be destroyed. "We are fully advised as to our status in case of war," wrote the representative of one company to the assistant secretary of state, "and that this property might be subject to confiscation or destruction by the Spanish Government." War between Spain and the United States, wrote the president of an-

other company, "will very likely mean the destruction of our valuable plant and in any event untold loss to our Company and its American stockholders." An American cork company with large interests in Spain; a New York merchant with trade in the Mediterranean and Black Sea; a Mobile firm which had chartered a Spanish ship to carry a cargo of timber — these are samples of American business interests which saw in war the threat of direct damage to themselves. They are hardly offset by the high hopes of an enterprising gentleman of Norfolk, "representing a party of capitalists who are enthusiastic supporters of the Government," who applied to the state department for a letter of marque "to enable us to lawfully capture Spanish merchant vessels and torpedo boats," adding: "We have secured option on a fine steam vessel and on receipt of proper documents will put to sea forthwith."

It seems safe to conclude, from the evidence available, that the only important business interests (other than the business of sensational journalism) which clamored for intervention in Cuba were certain of those directly or indirectly concerned in the Cuban sugar industry; that opposed to intervention were the influence of other parties (including at least one prominent sugar planter) whose business would suffer direct injury from war and also the overwhelming preponderance of general business opinion. After the middle of March, 1898, some conservative forces came to think intervention inevitable on humanitarian grounds, but many of the most influential business journals opposed it to the end.

II

We can now turn to the question whether American business was imperialistic; whether, in other words, business opinion favored schemes for acquiring foreign territory to supply it with markets, fields for capital investment, or commercial and naval stations in distant parts of the world. American business men were not unaware of the struggle for colonies then raging among European nations. Did they feel that the United States ought to participate in that struggle?

We have seen above that the rising tide of prosperity was intimately connected with the increase in American exports, particularly of manufactured articles. That the future welfare of American industry was dependent upon the command of foreign markets was an opinion so common as to appear almost universal. The New York *Journal of Commerce* pointed out, early in 1897, that the nation's industrial plant had been developed far beyond the needs of domestic consumption. In the wire nail industry there was said to be machinery to make four times as many nails as the American markets could consume. Rail mills, locomotive shops, and glass factories were in a similar situation. "Nature has thus destined this country for the industrial supremacy of the world," said the same paper later in the year. When the National Association of Manufacturers met in New York for its annual convention in January, 1898, "the discussion of ways and means for extending this country's trade, and more particularly its export business, was, in fact, almost the single theme of the speakers," according to *Bradstreet's*, which added the comment: "Nothing is more significant of the changed attitude toward this country's foreign trade, manifested by the American manufacturer today as compared with a few years ago, than the almost single devotion which he pays to the subject of possible export-trade extension."

But if business men believed, prior to the opening of the war with Spain, that foreign markets were to be secured through the acquisition of colonies, they were strangely silent about it. It cannot be said that the idea had not been brought to their attention. For almost a decade intellectual and political leaders such as Mahan, Albert Shaw, Murat Halstead, and Senators Lodge, Frye, and Morgan had been urging upon the country the need of an imperialistic program in the interest of its industrial and commercial development. The business world had, to all appearances, remained apathetic or frankly opposed to such a policy, which it regarded as simply one manifestation of dangerous jingoism. A large section of business opinion had, indeed, favored plans for the building of a Nicaraguan canal with governmental assistance, and some spokesmen for business had favored annexation of the Hawaiian Islands. But beyond these relatively modest projects, few business men, apparently, wished to go. Two of the most important commercial journals, the New York *Journal of Commerce* and the *Commercial and Financial Chronicle*, had stoutly opposed both the canal scheme and Hawaiian annexation. The former satirized the arguments of the proponents of both schemes. "We must certainly build the canal to defend the islands, and it is quite clear that we must acquire the islands . . . in order to defend the canal." The canal was not only unnecessary, but unless fortified at each end and patrolled by two fleets, it would be a positive misfortune. Such protection — "the price of jingoism" — might

easily cost us $25,000,000 a year, besides the lump sum that will be required for the original investment, and there is absolutely no excuse whatever in our commercial or our political interests for a single step in this long procession of expenses and of complications with foreign powers.

As for Hawaii and Cuba, neither was fit for self-government as a state — and the American constitution provided no machinery for governing dependencies. The Hawaiian Islands would have no military value unless the United States was to build a great navy and take an aggressive attitude in the Pacific. The *Commercial and Financial Chronicle* saw in colonies only useless outposts which must be protected at great expense, and the St. Louis *Age of Steel* warned lest the expansion of the export trade might "lead to territorial greed, as in the case of older nations, the price of which in armaments and militarism offsets the gain made by the spindle and the forge."

Colonies were not only certain to bear a fruit of danger and expense; they were valueless from the commercial point of view. Did not the colonies of Great Britain afford us one of the most valuable of our export markets? Did we not trade as advantageously with Guiana, a British colony, as with independent Venezuela? "Most of our ideas of the commercial value of conquests, the commercial uses of navies and the commercial advantages of political control," said the *Journal of Commerce,* dated back to times when colonial policies were designed to monopolize colonial trade for the mother country. The *Commercial and Financial Chronicle* believed that the current European enthusiasm for colonies was based on false premises; for although trade often followed the flag, "the trade is not always with the home markets of the colonizer. England and the United States are quite as apt to slip in with their wares under the very Custom-House pennant of the French or German dependency." Outright opposition, such as this, to the idea

of colonial expansion is not common in the business periodicals examined; much more common is complete silence on the subject. Positive and negative evidence together seem to warrant the conclusion that American business in general, at the opening of 1898, was either indifferent to imperialism or definitely opposed.

Confidence in the continued expansion of the export trade was based upon faith in the working of *laissez-faire* in a world given over largely to a system of free trade. American industry had reached a point where it could meet the world on more than even terms in both the price and the quality of its products. Given a fair chance, these products would make their own way. Government could aid them, not by acquiring colonial markets but by removing or lowering the barriers that restricted imports of raw materials and exchange commodities. To one who has in mind the subsequent tariff history of the United States, it is surprising to discover the amount of free-trade sentiment which found expression in these months of 1897–1898. The preoccupation of congress with the raising of duties in the Dingley Act was disturbing to those interested in the export trade. "It is pitiful," said the *Journal of Commerce,*

to see the national legislature bending its whole force to readjusting the trammels of a system which can only obstruct, and closing its eyes to the manifest, though unconscious, struggling of industry for a freedom that will enable it to compete successfully in any market of the world.

The futility of expecting to increase exports while at the same time barring out imports was stressed by more than one writer for business journals, and a change toward free trade in American policy was freely predicted. "We are gradually losing our fear of the bugaboo of cheap foreign labor," said the *Iron Age*, "and are slowly realizing that we hold the key of the position, since there are no indications that European manufacturers will ever displace us in the van of progress." The *American Machinist* declared that the recent growth in the export trade showed that in many lines the tariff was a dead letter, that goods which could be sold under the nose of the foreign producer no longer needed protection in the home market, and that the machinery interests would in all probability bring pressure to bear on Congress "toward action which will equalize these matters." The Chattanooga *Tradesman* was convinced that the great development in the export of manufactures was certain to have upon tariff policy an effect "both broad and radical," and the president of the Baltimore Chamber of Commerce, speaking on the same theme to that body in December, 1897, predicted that "the day is not so far distant when free trade, in some measure, at least, will become part of our political faith."

In a free-trade world, colonies would be of no importance. But if countries to which American producers looked for their markets should adopt restrictive policies, then a change in the American attitude might easily occur. Two events in the late fall of 1897 gave warning that the world at large might not continue hospitable to American products. The first was an address by Count Goluchowski, Austro-Hungarian Foreign Minister, to the Austro-Hungarian Delegations, in which he complained of the "destructive competition with transoceanic countries" and warned that the peoples of Europe "must fight shoulder to shoulder against the common danger, and must arm themselves for the struggle with all the means at their disposal." The twentieth century,

he declared, would be "a period marked by a struggle for existence in the politico-commercial sphere," and "the European nations must close their ranks in order successfully to defend their existence."

In the United States, the Austrian's pronouncement was generaly interpreted as aimed principally at this country. It caused widespread comment but little serious alarm. Many papers doubted the possibility of any European coöperation to exclude American products, pointing out that a stoppage of trade would injure Europe more than the United States, since we provided Europe with necessities in return for commodities most of which were either luxuries or articles that we could produce ourselves. Even if Europe should exclude our products, thought the New York *Commercial,* we should find an outlet in those other markets now cherished by Europe. This opinion was shared by the Philadelphia *Ledger,* which believed that, though concerted action in Europe might cripple our markets there, our trade with South America and the Far East could not "be directly disturbed through any European alliance." But the New York *Journal of Commerce,* in a thoughtful editorial, took a more serious view of the speech. In their determined quest for markets, it said, the industrial nations of Europe were following two courses: acquisition of colonies and the enactment of discriminatory tariffs. Hitherto each country had worked alone, but now there were signs of the rise of alliances or combinations in tariff policy. Since Austria-Hungary had a trade of but $10,000,000 a year with the United States, the idea put forward by Count Goluchowski must have been initiated elsewhere, and the paper suggested that a probable source was Russia, which had reason to seek to restrict the markets for American staples in both Europe and Asia.

The suspicion voiced by the *Journal of Commerce* that behind the Austrian's speech might lie concealed a threat to the American market in the Far East seemed partially confirmed within a few days, with the coming of news of European aggressions in China. Under the color of retaliation for the death of two German missionaries, a German force, on November 14, expelled the Chinese garrison at Tsingtau, at the mouth of Kiaochow Bay, seized the forts and occupied the port. Eight days later the German Government presented its formal demands, which included a naval station on Kiaochow Bay and the grant of the sole right to build railways and open coal mines in Shantung. By early in January, 1898, China had yielded all, and a convention to that effect was signed March 6. Meanwhile, within a week after the occupation of Tsingtau, Russian warships arrived at Port Arthur, and by May, 1898, China had agreed to the cession to Russia for twenty-five years of Port Arthur, Dalny, and other territory in the Liaotung peninsula. Compensating advantages were demanded and received by Great Britain and France, and by July 1, 1898, the partition of China had to all appearances begun.

Here were deeds more ominous than any words could be. They touched American business sentiment in a particularly sensitive spot, for though American trade with China was, in 1897, less than two per cent of its total foreign trade, exports to China in that year were almost double those of 1896, and there was a widespread belief that China was to provide an exceedingly important market for the surplus products of the United States. While some papers made light of the danger to American business presented by the Chinese crisis, and others professed to see positive advantage to the United States

in the development of China under European direction, the less optimistic saw a probability that American trade would find itself discriminated against or excluded altogether by the partitioning powers. Mr. Charles Denby, ex-Minister to China, in a note published in the *American Banker*, warned that with the seizure of territory, American commercial treaties with China "fall to the ground, and spheres of influence hostile to American commerce spring into existence." Similar alarm was voiced by numerous papers in all parts of the country, by none more vehemently than the New York *Journal of Commerce*. This paper, which has been heretofore characterized as pacifist, anti-imperialist, and devoted to the development of commerce in a free-trade world, saw the foundation of its faith crumbling as a result of the threatened partition of China. Declaring that free access to the markets of China, with its 400,000,000 people, would largely solve the problem of the disposal of our surplus manufactures, the *Journal* came out not only for a stern insistence upon complete equality of rights in China, but unreservedly also for an isthmian canal, the acquisition of Hawaii, and a material increase in the navy — three measures which it had hitherto strenuously opposed. Nothing could be more significant than the manner in which this paper was converted in a few weeks, justifying its change on each point by the needs of the hour in the Far East.

Finding the department of state, under Secretary Sherman, quite unimpressed by the seriousness of the Chinese situation, the *Journal of Commerce* itself initiated a movement to arouse the executive to a defence of American interests. At the paper's suggestion, a committee on American interests in China was organized in New York to work for concerted action by chambers of commerce in important cities. As a direct result of this propaganda, a committee of the Chamber of Commerce of the State of New York laid before that body on February 3, 1898, a report on "American Treaty Rights in China" and a memorial to the president of the United States. The report summarized the history of the acquisition of commercial rights through treaties with the Chinese Government and argued that those rights were seriously endangered by the recent aggressions of European powers. American products, it pointed out, were already virtually excluded from French Cochin China — an omen of what was to be expected elsewhere if France and other powers made good their positions on Chinese soil. "The Administration at Washington," the report continued,

seems to be supine about the present menace to those important interests of our citizens in China. . . . Under these circumstances it would seem that unless those concerned in our export trade take steps to agitate the matter and to have their interests safeguarded, nobody else will do it.

The memorial to the president, which was promptly adopted by the chamber, pictured the growing importance of American trade with China and the new dangers threatening it and respectfully urged that steps be taken

for the prompt and energetic defense of the existing treaty rights of our citizens in China, and for the preservation and protection of their important commercial interests in that Empire.

Within a few weeks similar action was taken by the chambers of commerce or boards of trade of Philadelphia, San Francisco, Baltimore, Boston, and Seattle. Not content with this action, a group of mer-

chants interested in the eastern trade held a meeting on March 3, at 59 Wall Street, New York, to form a permanent organization for the protection of that trade. A few days later, with the coöperation of the New York Chamber of Commerce, they took steps to organize the American China and Japan Association, to foster and safeguard the interests of citizens of the United States and others concerned in the trade with those empires and to secure and disseminate information relating thereto. The organization was not perfected until June 16. By that time the battle of Manila Bay had broadened the American outlook in the orient, and the organization followed suit, changing its title to the American Asiatic Association and including in its field of interest American trade not only in China and Japan, but also in "the Philippine Islands, and elsewhere in Asia and Oceania." Promptly upon its organization, the association put itself into communication with the department of state, offering its services for consultation or coöperation.

In the light of this widespread and intense interest in the preservation of the Chinese market, we can perhaps understand why American business, which had been to all appearances anti-war and anti-imperialist, was filled with sudden enthusiasm at the news of Dewey's victory at Manila Bay. Not only did the news dissipate all fears of a long and costly war and send stock prices rapidly upward; still more important, it seemed to place in American hands, all unexpectedly, the key to the trade of the orient. The attack on the Spanish fleet at Manila had been anticipated for months and well advertised by the American press. Some papers had speculated upon the value of the islands as an American colony and had foreseen that a victory there might greatly alter our relation to the imbroglio in

China. But for most, this thought did not occur until arrival of the news that the Spanish fleet was destroyed and Dewey safely in possession of Manila Bay. Then, at last, business men joined the jingoes in their acclaim of imperial conquests. Senator Lodge's exclamation — "We hold the other side of the Pacific, and the value to this country is almost beyond recognition" — was matched by many a formerly conservative business journal. It was not the intrinsic value of the Philippines or their trade that most impressed American writers, though this angle of the subject was not overlooked. Rather, their importance appeared to lie in their position as a gateway to the markets of eastern Asia.

It has been shown that the aggressions of the European powers in China had converted the New York *Journal of Commerce* to the belief that the United States must dig an isthmian canal, acquire Hawaii, and enlarge its navy. The same paper now took the lead in insisting that the newly won vantage point in the Philippines be retained and utilized to uphold American rights in China. However disconcerting might be our possession of Manila to European plans in the Far East, we must deal with it as a "factor in the protection of our interests in that part of the world." Hitherto we had

allowed Great Britain to fight our battle for an open market in China: with our flag floating within 500 miles of Hong Kong we shall be able to give that policy something more than merely moral support in the future.

There was thus "introduced a most formidable element of resistance to all that France and Russia at least seem to be working for in Asia." To return the islands to Spain or to dispose of them to England or any other power, said the same paper a few days later, "would be an act of inconceivable folly in the face of our imperative future necessities for a basis of naval and military force on the Western shores of the Pacific."

Endorsement of these views came rapidly from all sides. "Some broad-minded men," said the *Wall Street Journal*, May 5,

believe that the United States should retain enough interest in the Philippines to be sure of a coaling station and a naval base in Asiatic waters, under belief that the breaking up of China will make it necessary for this country to be in a position to protect, not only the existing trade with the far east, but the enormously greater trade likely to be developed in the next 25 years.

The *American Banker* of May 11, while absolving the United States from entering the war for any selfish purpose, declared that it could not relinquish the territories which it had been forced to seize, with the result that its diplomacy would no longer be a negative quantity in European counsels, "particularly not as respects the inevitable partition of the Chinese Empire. That a war with Spain," it added, "should have transpired at precisely this time, when Europe is tending to divide a considerable section of the inhabited earth, is a coincidence which has a providential air." The *Banker and Tradesman* likewise discerned the hand of Providence in bestowing the Philippines upon the United States at a time when Russia, France, and Germany were threatening American trade in China, and asked whether we could rightly throw away "a possession which would be of such great advantage to us in maintaining and defending our interests in this part of the globe." It asserted later that the answer to the question of the open door in China "was given, as European nations very well know, when Dewey entered Manila Bay and won his glorious victory." Similar views appeared in the *Age of Steel,* the *Iron Age,* the *United States Investor,* and the *Financial Record. Bradstreet's* thought the possession of Manila would greatly accelerate the growth of American trade in Asia and predicted that that city "might in time even rival Hong Kong as a distributive trade center." The New York *Commercial,* using figures supplied by the bureau of statistics in Washington, pointed out that countries closely adjacent to the Philippines contained 850,000,000 people and purchased over one billion dollars worth of goods a year, mostly articles grown or manufactured in the United States. "With the Philippines as a three-quarter way house, forming a superb trading station, the bulk of this trade should come to this country." The New York Chamber of Commerce, in a report on "American Interests in China," argued that, in face of the prospect that European spheres of influence in China might become permanent territorial acquisitions, the only course by which the United States could protect its interests appeared to be active participation in politics on the "dangerous ground of the Far East"—a participation which might be "hastened and materialized through our possible occupation of the Philippine Islands."

The insistence that the Philippines be retained, for the sake of their own trade and as a gateway to Asiatic markets, was confined to no one section of the country. In the south, business men saw in possession of the islands assurance of the continued growth of the marketing of American cotton goods in China. The Pacific Coast, very naturally, displayed a lively interest. In Dewey's victory the *Mining and Scientific Press* saw an earnest that the coast cities would be transformed from the back door to the front door of civilization. "The guns that destroyed the Spanish fleet in Manila Bay thundered a warning to the nations of our approaching commercial supremacy in the Orient." The *Commercial Bulletin of Southern California* believed acquisition of the Philippines would greatly hasten the growth of trans-Pacific trade and asserted it was with this expectation that "Pacific Coast people so generally favor territorial expansion." The *Daily Commercial News and Shipping List,* of San Francisco, thought the coast people would make determined efforts for the retention of the Philippines. The Chamber of Commerce of Seattle and the Chamber of Commerce, Merchants' Association, and Manufacturers' and Producers' Association of San Francisco petitioned the president to retain not only the Philippines, but the Caroline and Ladrone Islands, "and all other lands which are now, or may hereafter be acquired in the present war with Spain," in the interests of humanity and the Oriental trade of the United States. Even James J. Hill, who had been a strong opponent of the war, stated to a newspaper reporter that if it rested with him, he would retain the Philippines. "If you go back in the commercial history of the world," he was reported as saying, "you will find that the people who controlled the trade of the Orient have been the people who held the purse strings of nations."

It must not be inferred that business opinion was unanimous in favor of retaining the Philippines. There was an undercurrent of opposition or indifference. The New York *Journal of Commerce,* just before the signing of the peace protocol, deplored the fact that timid people were shrinking from imperialism and that "the business men of the country are maintaining a deathlike silence." The *Commercial and Financial Chronicle* was cautious, pointing out that Spain's distant possessions had proved its most vulnerable point — a fact from which the United States might learn a lesson — and hoping that the United States might yet find a way to avoid such a dangerous responsibility. The Baltimore *Journal of Commerce* was, in July, strongly opposed to annexation, and two months later held that no one yet knew whether "our position as wetnurse to Cuba, proprietors of Porto Rico and pantata to the Philippines is likely to bring us profit or loss." The *Iron Age*, which early in the summer had been strongly for expansion, was by September harboring qualms as to the real value of colonies to the business man. Everett Frazar, president of the American Asiatic Association, was personally a warm supporter of annexation, but the association held upon its table for months without action a resolution on the subject. The San Francisco *Call*, representing the California Hawaiian sugar interests of the Spreckels family, was strongly opposed to annexation, arguing not only that Anglo-Saxons had no aptitude for tropical colonization, but also frankly warning California sugar-beet growers of the danger of competition from Philippine cane-sugar.

There is no way of measuring accurately the strength of business opinion for and against the retention of the Philippines. Judging opinion as best we could from the available expressions of it, it seemed safe to conclude that American business in the winter of 1897–1898 was opposed to war and either opposed to colonial expansion or oblivious to the existence of the problem. From similar evidence it seems equally safe to conclude that after the battle of Manila Bay American business became definitely imperialistic — that is, if a wish to retain the Philippines is an evidence of an imperialistic attitude. It seems certain, too, from the

prominence given to the Chinese situation in nearly every discussion of the value of the islands, that the conversion of business opinion was accomplished by the combination of a European threat against the freedom of the American market in China, present and prospective, with the dramatic *coup* of the American fleet in a fine harbor so near the Chinese coast. In one paper, the New York *Journal of Commerce,* there appears with beautiful clarity the shift of position induced by the action of the European Powers in China. In November, 1897, against all schemes of colonial or naval expansion; in December, for a canal, Hawaiian annexation, and a big navy; in May and thereafter, for retention of the entire Philippine archipelago and aggressive assertion of American rights in China — the *Journal* reveals a process of thought which perhaps occurred less clearly and consciously in the minds of many business men.

Having concluded that the Philippines were wholesome and digestible, business was disposed to treat itself to more of the same diet. The venture in the Philippines strengthened immeasurably the demand for the annexation of Hawaii. "The battle of Manila Bay," said the *Journal of Commerce* May 31, "makes it imperative that we should establish permanent arrangements which will make the [Hawaiian] islands a halfway house on the road to the Philippines." When the joint resolution for annexation passed congress and received the president's signature on July 7, it was hailed not only as good in itself and in relation to the Philippines, but as the first actual step on the path of imperialism. The resolution, thought *Bradstreet's,* "gave a new direction to the impulse toward expansion, which is seldom missing among the characteristics of great nations." But there were other Pacific islands that beckoned. "Bridge the Pacific!" cried the Philadelphia *Press*. "With the Philippines go the Carolines, a Spanish possession; Samoa and the Hawaiian Islands complete the chain." The war in the Pacific, the prospect of new possessions there, and the voyage of the *Oregon* also gave new force to the demand for an isthmian canal. In the Caribbean, business interests not only insisted that the United States needed Porto Rico for its strategic and commercial value, but suggested that it might prove impossible to adhere to the Teller Amendment, which had pledged the United States not to annex Cuba. The *Journal of Commerce*, voicing skepticism as to the capacity of the Cubans for orderly government, declared: "The Teller amendment . . . must be interpreted in a sense somewhat different from that which its author intended it to bear." The American flag must float over Cuba until law and order were assured. American covetousness in the Caribbean was not limited to the Spanish islands. As early as March 31, 1898, the New York *Commercial* had advocated the purchase of St. Thomas, in the Danish West Indies, for a naval base. In May, it saw signs that the British West Indies might be interested in coming under the American flag and urged that the Bahamas, Jamaica, and Bermuda be not lost sight of during the war. The *Journal of Commerce*, endorsing the same idea, remarked:

Our people are now in an expansive mood and there is a deep and strong American sentiment that would rejoice to see the British flag, as well as the Spanish flag, out of the West Indies.

Merchants and manufacturers now saw in colonies a partial solution of the disposal of the surplus of American products. European countries, prejudiced against our goods, said the New York *Commercial* (evidently recalling Count Goluchowski's speech), had acquired colonial markets while we had none; but the acquisition of the Spanish islands would supply the lack; their development by American capital would stimulate the demand for the products of our fields and factories. We should regulate their customs in a manner to favor our own industries and shipping and discourage those of other countries. This procedure was condemned by the *Journal of Commerce*, the *Commercial and Financial Chronicle*, and other journals and organizations, which insisted that after urging the "open door" in China we must adhere to the same principle in our new possessions. But whether the door was to be open or closed to the rest of the world, an active and lucrative trade with the new possessions was widely anticipated. "One way of opening a market is to conquer it . . ." said the *Railway World* in August. "Already our enterprising merchants are beginning to organize to take possession of the markets which our army and navy have opened to them." The Chicago *Inter-Ocean*, in a series of interviews with merchants and manufacturers in several cities, found them

very generally waking up to the opportunities which the war has brought at a moment when the immense increase of our manufacturing capacity has rendered foreign outlets absolutely necessary to us.

The bureau of statistics reported large numbers of inquiries from all parts of the country, but chiefly from the great producing and business centers, as to the imports of Cuba and Porto Rico. Not only the trade prospects but also the opportunities for American capital and skill to develop the resources of the islands excited enthusiasm. A national bank of Hawaii was organized immediately after passage of the annexation resolution. Similar plans were afoot for Porto Rico and Cuba, and enterprising Americans were studying financial conditions in the Philippines. "Railroad building may be expected to boom in all the islands which may fall under the influence of the United States," said the *Rand-McNally Bankers' Monthly.* Cane sugar and tobacco growing would receive an impetus. "The forests may also be made to yield handsome returns, . . . and in fact every industry, so long under the blighting rule of Spain, will be exploited and made to show the advantages accruing from better government and wider enterprise."

American business had yielded reluctantly to the necessity of a war with Spain, forced upon the United States by the distressing situation in Cuba. It had not foreseen, or if it foresaw had feared, the colonial responsibilities to which such a war might lead. But when Dewey's dramatic victory on the first of May offered a far eastern base from which the threatened markets in China might be defended, it had gladly accepted the result, and long before the close of the wonderful year 1898 it was building high hopes upon the supposed opportunities for trade and exploitation in a string of dependencies stretching from the Philippines to Porto Rico. As the year expired, spokesmen of the business and financial interests of the country were hailing the "incalculable expansion of the influence of the United States among other nations," or declaring philosophically that the year had "witnessed a complete change in the temper and aspirations of the American people." . . . "Our commercial horizon has been broadened," said one of them,

our ideas of the work which is before us have been greatly magnified, and we have begun to be slightly conscious of the field of development into which this nation is evidently destined to enter.

In no section of American opinion had the year wrought a greater transformation than in that of the business men.

Joseph E. Wisan: THE CUBAN CRISIS AS REFLECTED IN THE NEW YORK PRESS

THE decade of the 1890's which witnessed the final crisis of the long continued friction between Spain and her Cuban colony marked also the appearance of a new type of journalism in New York City. While a number of veteran newspaper men were grimly attempting to maintain conservative standards, a new school in newspaper making with its reckless headlines, "popular" features, and sensational appeals to the masses reached many readers previously impervious to the comparatively staid sheets of the old order.

In only one important respect were the old and the new journalists similar — in

From Joseph E. Wisan, *The Cuban Crisis as Reflected in the New York Press* (1895–1898) (New York: Columbia University Press, 1934), pp. 21–26, 33–34, 187–190, 233–234, 390–395, 455–460. Used by permission.

the manner in which the policy and conduct of the paper were dominated by an outstanding individual. "So intimately and completely did his personality pervade the *Sun* that throughout the country it was quite as customary to hear people say 'Dana says so' as 'the *Sun* says so,' a kind of public recognition of the individual force of the editor." This might have been said, more aptly in 1895, of Pulitzer and the *World*, Godkin and the *Evening Post*, Hearst and the *Journal*. Dana had ceased to be the all-powerful directing genius of earlier years; Pulitzer was in his very prime; Hearst just making his start in the East; and Godkin, despite increasing years, as active as ever.

In 1895 the important metropolitan morning newspapers were the *World*, the *Journal*, the *Sun*, the *Herald*, the *Tribune*, and the *Times;* the leading evening sheets were the *Evening Post*, the *Commercial Advertiser*, and the *Mail and Express*. The *Journal of Commerce* represented the financial and commercial elements.

The *World* was owned by Joseph Pulitzer, whose career in the field of journalism had been most unusual. An ambitious immigrant in 1864, Pulitzer had served in many humble occupations. His newspaper experience began in Carl Schurz's *Westliche Post* in which he later bought an interest. He was employed by the New York *Sun*, purchased the St. Louis *Evening Post* which he transformed into the *Post-Dispatch*, and, in 1833, bought the *World* from Jay Gould. The newspaper was in poor shape when the change in ownership occurred. Pulitzer made a remarkable success of the enterprise. He created a new type of journal, "a journal that is not only cheap but bright, not only bright but large, not only large but truly democratic — dedicated to the cause of the people rather than of purse-potentates — devoted more to the

New than the Old World — that will expose all fraud and sham, fight all public evils and abuses — that will serve and battle for the people with earnest sincerity." A week later his platform appeared — taxation of luxuries, of inheritances, of large incomes, of monopolies and privileged corporations, a tariff for revenue, civil service reform, punishment for corruption in office, vote buying and political coercion. Pulitzer employed every device to interest new readers. Screaming headlines, lurid style, profuse illustrations disgusted conservative readers but swelled circulation. Pulitzer outdid the earlier efforts of the Bennetts and the appearance of Hearst as an arch rival for the patronage of the lower classes compelled a reluctant adoption of even more spectacular methods.

Sensational handling of the news, however, was not Pulitzer's sole contribution. As the champion of the downtrodden he undertook many crusades. These reforms were advocated in his striking editorial page, and to Pulitzer that page was the paper. One of his secretaries records: "It is no exaggeration to say that the editorial page of the *World* was to Joseph Pulitzer what a child is to a parent."

A Democrat since 1876, Pulitzer had supported Cleveland in 1884, 1888, and 1892, yet he took sharp issue with the President in several important instances. The *World* believed Cleveland too close to Wall Street; it denounced the sale of bonds to the Morgan-Rothschild syndicate early in 1895 and the failure to prosecute the trusts. It criticized Cleveland's Venezuela message as jingoistic and advocated peace. Olney it detested.

The *World* boasted a capable staff — Bradford Merrill, managing editor until shortly after the *Maine* was torpedoed, E. O. Chamberlain, James Mark Tuohy, London correspondent and chief of the foreign service, Nelson S. Cobleigh, who as foreign editor had charge of all Cuban news, J. J. Eakins, city editor, and James Creelman.

Pulitzer's success with the *World* may be gauged by its increase in circulation. In 1883 the eight-page paper sold about 15,000 copies daily. In 1895 the sixteen page *World*, selling for the same price of two cents, boasted a circulation of 555,570 daily. For the year 1896, the *World* claimed an average weekday circulation of 743,024 and an average Sunday circulation of 562,903. According to its own statement there had been an average increase of 182,934 in the weekday issues and of 176,287 in the Sunday paper. By 1898 the circulation reached over five million copies per week, "the largest of any newspaper printed in any language in any country."

William Randolph Hearst, Pulitzer's chief rival, began his career in New York journalism on September 25, 1895, when, at the age of thirty, he purchased the New York *Morning Journal* from John R. McLean. Hearst's wealthy father had given him control in 1887 of the San Francisco *Examiner*, a newspaper the elder Hearst had taken over for a bad debt some years before. Hearst succeeded in making a financial success of the sheet, raising its circulation from almost nothing to 80,000 in a city of 300,000. This success he achieved by adopting sensational methods copied, generally, from Pulitzer. It was Hearst's ambition to surpass Pulitzer in sensationalism, circulation, and power, and his entrance into New York journalism began an intense rivalry between the two papers.

Hearst reduced the price of the *Journal* to one cent and improved its staff by transfers from his San Francisco *Examiner* and by acquisition from his New York rivals. Associated with him at various times were Creelman, Grover Flint, Cuban correspondent with Gómez's army for four months, Alfred Henry Lewis, Washington correspondent, Julian Hawthorne, Richard Harding Davis, Karl Decker, Frederic Remington, and George Eugene Bryson. Melodrama, crime, vice, advice to the lovelorn, bizarre treatment of alleged scientific discoveries, became "news"; or, as the *Journal* described it, "true stories of the new romances, mystery, pathos and humor caught from the whirl of everyday life." The *Journal* ran theatrical benefits for the city's poor; it offered rewards for the capture of notorious criminals; it interviewed kings; it hired prominent men for special assignments. A favorite trick was to wire statesmen for their views on important questions and to broadcast their replies conspicuously. A special Hoe color press, making possible an eight-page comic section for the Sunday *Journal*, was installed. Streamer headlines, introduced in the Sunday *Journal*, were later adopted by the daily.

In international affairs Hearst invariably adopted an anti-foreign attitude. Spain, England, France, Japan, China, were all attacked for purposes of circulation.

In 1897 the *Journal* was increased in size, the regular edition being supplemented by a "magazine" devoted to "science in popular form, news of the week, and human interest," and a 24 page woman's supplement. The Easter Sunday edition in 1897 reached 116 pages; a special Christmas edition, 112. This was rendered possible by an amazing growth in circulation. Hearst claimed an average daily increase of 1500 new readers during the first year of his proprietorship. The paper advertised an increase from 77,239 to 430,410 for the daily and 54,308 to 408,779 for the Sunday edition. On the day following McKinley's election the *Morning Journal* printed 956,921 copies. This, Hearst declared, was "an achievement not only unparalleled in the history of the world but hitherto undreamed-of in the realm of modern journalism." During each of the three days following the destruction of the *Maine,* the *Journal* printed over a million copies. After Dewey's victory at Manila its circulation exceeded 1,600,000 and it remained well over 1,250,000 during the war. . . .

The influence of the New York newspapers upon the nation at large was very great. The *World, Journal, Sun,* and *Herald,* all with special correspondents in Cuba, sold their news service to papers outside the city. The Chicago *Tribune* used the *World* service and also the *Journal* syndicate service; the Boston *Herald* and Chicago *Times-Herald* secured the New York *Herald* service; the San Francisco *Chronicle* took both the New York *Herald* and the *Sun* services; and the San Francisco *Examiner,* a Hearst paper, was furnished the same service as the *Journal.* Furthermore, since all the leading New York newspapers except the *Sun* were members of the Associated Press their news was available for transmission to other member papers.

A study of *Public Opinion* for the period from February, 1895 to April, 1898 shows that of 181 excerpts quoted from the nation's newspapers concerning Cuban affairs, the New York press furnished 56.

The outbreak of the Cuban revolution came at an opportune time for the newspapers. For twenty years no other foreign event had aroused sustained interest. The American people were confident of their prowess; the generation since the Civil War had witnessed enormous material progress. An intense national consciousness and belief in manifest destiny had accompanied these material advances. Public opinion could easily be enlisted behind an aggressive foreign policy. Spain was a decadent nation. Americans shared the belief that the traditions and policies of the Spanish monarchy were obsolete, cruel, and oppressive. Also, Cuba lay close to our shores. A deep and continued interest in the island had been felt since the early days of the Republic. A large trade and American investments in Cuba strengthened our historic and sentimental interest. Moreover, most Americans sympathized heartily with the desire of a western people to achieve independence of a European monarchy. And finally, the methods adopted by the Spanish government to combat the rebellion were ill understood in this country; the temperament of the Castilian nation was even less understood. All the elements necessary for the creation of "good copy" were at hand, and the sensational press made the most of its opportunity. . . .

The sensational press treatment of the multifarious phases of the Cuban crisis was due only in part to the nature of the events themselves. Much of it resulted from the development of the "new journalism," the roots of which lay in the past, but which reached full development during the years 1897–1898.

The typical new journal was jealous of its power; it was proud of itself and of its circulation, of which it blatantly boasted. It spent money lavishly. It hired special correspondents for important assignments. It "did things" as well as wrote about them. It was contemptuous of its rivals.

The *Journal* offered the most conspicuous example of this attitude and policy. Anxious to wrest circulation leadership from Pulitzer's *World,* it spared no expense to furnish exciting news. To its already costly staff covering the Cuban situation, it added Richard Harding Davis and Frederic Remington for special service.

Davis's special articles frequently occupied five first-page columns. One, together with Remington's illustrations, describing the execution of a brave young Cuban, Rodríguez, covered all the first page and half of the second. Davis's work moved the *Commercial Advertiser* to anger, and the *Mail and Express* to praise.

Creelman's articles from Madrid were also prominently featured. The reputation of their author, his undoubted ability, and the vehemence and vigor of his style made his reports exceptionally good copy. Many editorials were based directly upon Creelman's dispatches.

A series of half a dozen special articles by Senator-elect Money, special *Journal* "Commissioner," shared front page honors in January. Bryson and Rodriguez managed also to obtain first page space. A *Journal* correspondent, Ralph D. Paine, accompanied a filibustering expedition of the *Three Friends* and described his experiences.

The *Journal* was the first newspaper to send to Cuba its own dispatch boat, the *Vamoose*. This was done in order to counteract the effects of Weyler's rigid censorship. It boasted that the *Vamoose* was "the fastest boat in American waters," and that, despite De Lome's efforts to delay the progress of her mission to Cuba, she would get the news.

The *Journal* ridiculed the attempts of the other newspapers to keep up with it. It scoffed at "the sneers and snarls of the tired representatives of the old journalism attempting to discredit the *Journal's* exclusive news." The close relationship between the development of the new journalism and the Cuban crisis is well illustrated in an editorial boasting of its priority in reporting the contemplated grant of autonomy. "No matter of international discussion interests the people of the United States more than the struggle of the Cubans for liberty. . . . Recognizing the existence of this universal interest, the *Journal* has spared no pains and no expense in its effort to gather and publish every piece of trustworthy information on the subject. It has sent to Cuba from time to time correspondents who represent the highest journalistic, military, political, literary or artistic attainments. It dispatched to Madrid Mr. James Creelman who antedated by sixteen days the *Herald's* instructive 'news' of yesterday. To those eminent exponents of the old journalism, the *Herald*, which copies after sixteen days the news the *Journal* obtained from headquarters at Madrid, and the *World*, which positively contradicted statements of fact which the *Herald* now affirms, the *Journal* presents its compliments and promises to leave them to the uninterrupted practice of their style of newspaper making. The new journalism prints what is new and prints it first."

The *World*, in an attempt to counteract the *Journal's* methods, claimed a series of scoops. In this Scovel was its greatest asset, although Dr. Bowen continued to send extremely good reports from the field. Pulitzer claimed an exclusive Gómez interview obtained at Gómez's camp near Salado, Santa Clara, in which the Cuban general denied his willingness to accept autonomy for the island. Its cruelty-affidavit scoops of early December it considered a real achievement. It prided itself upon an exclusive Weyler statement denying the charge that Maceo had been assassinated. It claimed to have presented "the first authentic news of the movements of the Cuban patriot armies that has reached New York in many weeks."

This service was due, according to the *World*, to the "unrivalled skill and daring of its correspondent with the patriots, Sylvester Scovel," who "combines all the great and high qualities of the war correspondent — devotion to duty, accuracy, graphic descriptive power, absolute courage and skill." It reported the special gratitude of the Cuban Junta for its exposé of Spanish massacres. It capitalized Ona Melton's appeal to it for aid. It claimed that its Madrid dispatch gave the fullest information of the home rule offer. It asserted that Bowen was the only correspondent permitted to pass beyond Artemisa and featured his description of conditions in that area. It made the most of Scovel's imprisonment, continuing to print his despatches and increasing its circulation by about 8000 during one month.

When subjected to criticism the Pulitzer and Hearst newspapers seemed pleased. A Havana newspaper having published a three-column attack on the American press, charging it with a systematic attempt to deceive, the *World* expressed pleasure that it had been singled out for particular criticism. When Weyler blamed the "pernicious activity" of the newspapers of the United States for his failure to subdue the insurgents earlier, the *Journal* applauded his "tribute to the press," and declared, "it is a grateful compliment. . . . It is true that the press of this country has done what it could to create public sentiment against the infamous cruelty of the Spanish pirate in Cuba and in favor of intervention by this government." The *Evening Post* reported that Spanish officials in Puerto Rico destroyed American newspapers whenever they could find them. . . .

Much space was still accorded to reports of Spanish cruelty. The execution of prisoners of war, starvation, the plun-der and murder of defenseless pacificos, the inhuman treatment of women, attacks upon hospitals, the poisoning of wells, and the killing of children, were constantly in the news. The Spaniards were also accused of several new forms of deviltry. An article in the *Journal* charged a Spanish colonel with arranging for the sale of ten Cuban children, the crime being exposed by a local priest. Another in the same paper described the imprisonment of nuns. The *Mail and Express* was moved to editorial horror by the report that a minor Spanish butcher — one Fondeviella — "murdered without cause, three Cuban youths guilty of the crime of playing the American game of baseball, and when the mothers and sisters of the victims tearfully begged permission to bury the bodies, snarled: 'The bodies of Cubans are fit only to feed dogs.'" The *Journal* repeated the story several days later. In an editorial recapitulating the forms of Spanish cruelty, the *Journal* suggested that Spain might find it necessary to inoculate Cuban prisoners with smallpox germs and release them to mingle freely with their fellows. The deportation to Fernando Po, with civil trial, of members of secret societies, especially the Cuban Masonic Lodges, was reported in the *World*. The same paper asserted that Weyler's reinstatement to power of Carreras and Olavarrieta, the two killers whose removal, the preceding June, the *World* claimed to have effected by its publicity campaign, meant "a virtual massacre." The *Journal* was particularly active in January in exposing Spanish cruelty. Several articles by Senator-elect Money dealt with the subject, as did a series of drawings by Remington. Money repeated most of the accusations already referred to — the summary execution of sick and wounded taken from hospitals, the waging of warfare against women, and outrages on pacificos; Remington's drawings represented the sacking of a hospital, the arrest of pacificos and the like. . . .

The sensational newspapers were fully alive to the public's excited interest in the [sinking of the *Maine*] and to the opportunity offered to themselves, and made frantic efforts to get — or manufacture — the news, and to present it in the most lurid fashion. During the week beginning February 17th, the *Journal* devoted a daily average space of 8½ pages to the *Maine* — news, editorials, and pictures. It sent the yachts *Buccaneer* and *Anita* and the tug *Echo* to Havana, and massed at the Cuban capital its group of special correspondents — Hawthorne, Decker, Creelman, Lewis, Bryson, and artists Remington and Bengough. It offered a reward of fifty thousand dollars "for the conviction of the criminals who sent 258 American sailors to their death." Declaring that "the government has set an investigation on foot, and the *Journal* has independently undertaken another," it boasted, "between them the truth will soon be known." It inaugurated a fund to build a monument in memory of the *Maine* victims, associating with itself in this endeavor many names prominent in civil and military life, including Levi P. Morton, General Miles, Rear Admiral Selfridge, O. H. P. Belmont, George Gould, Depew, and General O. O. Howard. The *World* chartered a special tug and engaged divers to investigate the wreck, and was disappointed when refused permission to do so. According to its own figures the *Journal's* circulation for the week of January 9th had averaged 416,885; on February 17th it reached 1,025,624; on February 18th, 1,036,140. For the week beginning February 27th the average figure was 632,217.

The news columns of Hearst's paper seemed deliberately intended to inflame the public. "The warship *Maine* was split in two by an enemy's secret infernal machine"; "Captain Sigsbee practically declares that his ship was blown up by a mine or a torpedo"; "Strong evidence of crime"; "There are many among the Spanish officers and privates who hate Americans to the point of frenzy"; "If this can be proven, the brutal nature of the Spaniards will be shown in that they waited to spring the mine until after all men had retired for the night. The Maltese Cross [referring to an accompanying illustration] shows where the mine may have been fired." One leading headline read, "THE WHOLE COUNTRY THRILLS WITH WAR FEVER." The governors of many states reported the readiness and anxiety of the militia for service. One picture was captioned, "Divers searching for the dead and the evidence that they were murdered under the murky waters of Havana Bay." On February 20th (the day the Court of Inquiry left for Havana to begin its investigation) the *Journal* presented "proof of a submarine mine." Under a headline, "HAVANA POPULACE INSULTS THE MEMORY OF THE MAINE VICTIMS," appeared the statement that Spanish officers had boasted that any other American ship visiting Havana would "follow the *Maine*." "THE MAINE WAS DESTROYED BY TREACHERY" was another headline. A few days later Karl Decker claimed to have "the secret testimony on which the Court of Inquiry will base its portentous report." The *Journal* quoted authorities (far removed from Havana) to prove its contention that the explosion was external and deliberate — Assistant Secretary Roosevelt, Chief Constructor Philip Hichborn, Rear Admiral George E. Belknap (retired), and Naval Constructor Bolles. Captain Zalinski (a retired naval officer

and "dynamite expert") judged from the
Journal's photographs that a mine blew
up the *Maine*. The Italian ex-Premier
Crispi's opinion that the *Maine's* destruction was not accidental was made the
subject of a leading editorial.

Though the *World* did not quite match
its rival's sensationalism, it adopted similar tactics. Turning from its earlier headline guesses that "The *Maine* explosion
was caused by a bomb" and that there
was "Suspicion of a torpedo," and empha-
sizing the work of its own special investigators, it announced on February 20th
that the "*World's* discoveries prove the
mine theory." Another headline read,
"War spirit rising from *World's* evidence."
And still another, "Government accepts
mine theory of *World*." It featured a
report that Sigsbee had attributed the
explosion to external forces. It warned of
the damage possible from the guns of the
Vizcaya, expected to arrive that day.
"While lying off the Battery, her shells
will explode on the Harlem River and in
the suburbs of Brooklyn." A full page
streamer announced that the President
and Congress were "ready for action." It
described the elaborate preparations of
the Government to improve the Atlantic
Coast defense and insisted that we were
fully prepared for war. A large picture
representing American cannon pointed at
the *Vizcaya* accompanied this article.

The *World* and *Journal* differed widely
in their editorial treatment of the event.
Though the *Journal* did not believe that
the *Maine's* destruction had been ordered
officially by Spain, it demanded that the
"execrable assassination" of the vessel
should lead to the immediate recognition
of Cuban independence. It devoted a
series of editorials urging American intervention to gain that end. "The investigation . . . may take a week but the independence of Cuba can be recognized

today." Accidental or not, the *Maine's*
destruction would have been prevented
had Cuban independence been recognized before as the *Journal* had advised.
"If we had stopped the war in Cuba when
duty and policy alike urged us to do, the
Maine would have been afloat today, and
three hundred homes now desolate would
have been unscathed. . . . It would never
have happened if there had been peace
in Cuba, as there would have been if we
had done our duty." Sharing fully in the
guilt were those responsible for our policies of non-recognition and non-intervention. To those men the *Journal* issued a
direct challenge. "If it be found that the
Spanish authorities have brought about
this calamity . . . no power from the White
House to Wall Street will be able to re-
strain the American people." "President
Hanna . . . announced that there will be
no war. . . . This attitude is fairly representative of the eminently respectable
porcine citizens who — for dollars in the
money-grubbing sty, support 'conservative' newspapers and consider the starvation of . . . inoffensive men, women and
children, and the murder of 250 American sailors . . . of less importance than a
fall of two points in a price of stocks."
"Let the administration wake up, and let
Congress throw off the incubus of Reed,
Hale, Boutelle . . . and in the name of
common sense and patriotism, let us have
a Secretary of the Navy who is not a grad-
uate of the Peace Society."

The *World's* first editorial was quite
pacific. It advised that the *Vizcaya's* visit
be delayed. It recapitulated the history
of former accidents to iron-clads and
criticized the policy of building ships of
such doubtful value. It demanded a
speedy investigation and, in fact, pro-
tested against the apparent apathy of the
Government in its efforts to fix the cause
of the explosion. Though it did not advo-

cate war if the explosion was proved to have been the act of an irresponsible Spaniard, it would hold Spain to account, contending that even if the act had been committed by an insurgent Cuban, she was at fault. It asked Spain to cooperate with the United States Government and the "conservative press" to allay public excitement by an official denial that the *Maine* had been anchored over a mine. Though admitting that "nobody outside of a lunatic asylum" asserted that "Spain officially blew up the *Maine*," it rejected Weyler's emphatic insistence that no mines had been placed in Havana Har-

bor. As Scovel reported evidence pointing to an external explosion, it considered more fully the nature of Spanish reparations, deciding finally that only the liberation of Cuba would suffice. "Whether Spanish treachery devised, or Spanish willingness permitted this colossal crime, Spain is responsible for it. . . . No number of millions of mere money could make return for the cowardly slaughter of these brave men and treacherous destruction of a noble ship. The only atonement at all adequate for such a deed would be the liberation of Cuba." If Spain refused, war must necessarily follow. . . .

CONCLUSION

The Spanish-American War, so momentous in its consequences, was a popular crusade. Neither the business interests of the nation nor the Government executives desired it. The public, aroused by the press, demanded it.

The leading commercial and financial interests of the nation favored an early restoration of stability in Cuba. They sought not only to avoid war, but to minimize its possibility. Investors in Cuban enterprises, anxious above all else to restore the security of their properties, attributed their losses to the tactics of the insurgents, and opposed all direct or indirect aid to them. Edwin F. Atkins, one of the leading American investors in Cuba, and influential with high officials of both the Cleveland and McKinley Administrations, sought constantly to prevent such aid. Indeed, he was accused of poisoning Olney's mind against the insurgents. General industrial and banking interests, emerging from the serious depression of 1893, and anxious to permit the unhampered operation of McKinley's policies, feared the possible effects of war. Furthermore, the 1896 campaign had not

ended the menace of free silver; a war, possibly prolonged and certain to be costly, would strengthen the position of the silverites. It was no mere accident that most of the leading proponents of intervention in Congress represented southern and western states where populism and silver were strongest.

Wall Street served as a sensitive index of the fears of the financial interests. Rumors of increased tension in Spanish-American relations were almost invariably accompanied by a decline in stock prices and by editorial demands for peace from financial organs. Examples of this tendency may be seen in the falling prices which resulted from the Senate's adoption of the belligerency resolutions (Feb. 29, 1896), the conviction of the *Competitor* prisoners (May 12, 1896), a report that the St. Louis convention would demand armed intervention in Cuba (June 18, 1896), the Maceo assassination story December 15, 1896), the Senate Committee on Foreign Relations' adoption of the Cameron resolution (December 19, 1896), the publicity given to the views of Hannis Taylor (November 5, 1897), the destruction of the *Maine* (February 16, 1898), and the passage of the $50,000,000 defense bill (March 7, 1898). On the other hand, reports of incidents making for peace between the two nations rallied prices. For example, gains were recorded when Cleveland indicated a strong desire to adjust our difficulties amicably (March 10, 1896, April 14, 1896), when Madrid ordered a postponement of the execution of the *Competitor* prisoners (May 13, 1896), and when Olney announced that Cleveland would not be bound by the Congressional Resolution of December, 1896 (December 20, 1896; December 22, 1896). Mark Hanna's determined opposition to the war is typical of the attitude of the nation's leading business men. The *Journal of Commerce* consistently opposed American intervention.

Spain's inability to protect American property in Cuba was annoying, as were the hindrances she imposed upon American commerce during the early part of the insurrection. However, during the later stages of the revolt she did everything possible to offer protection and she removed the curbs on American business in Cuba. American claims for damages could have been settled easily with a nation striving to maintain peace. Spanish historians, such as Maura and Ortega, attach little significance to this aspect of the controversy between the two nations, condemning American Jingoes, not American business men, as the provokers of an unjustifiable war. Indeed, the most bitter complaints of Spain's interferences with American business came from the ranks of the Jingoes thirsting for war, not from among the business men whose financial interests were immediately involved.

Responsible officials of both the Cleveland and McKinley Administrations strove to avoid an open break. Energetic and generally effective steps were taken to prevent filibustering. Cleveland's proclamations of neutrality, his repeated criticism of American mediation towards a permanent solution in which Spanish sovereignty would be safeguarded, his anxiety to obtain from the Supreme Court a decision setting clearly defined legal limits to filibustering operations, all bespeak his efforts on behalf of peace. Despite an increasing irritation at Spain's inability to restore peace, he and Olney were a constant bulwark against the Jingoes. McKinley, more responsive to popular and party demands, and willing to add to the prestige of his Administration by minor diplomatic victories, was equally anxious to avoid war, as was his entire cabinet, with the exception of Alger. Despite the presence of bellicose individuals such as Lodge and Roosevelt, the force of Republican leadership was exerted for peace. Woodford's sincere efforts to maintain peace during March and April, 1898, were undertaken to please and help his superiors, not to make their position more awkward. McKinley's problem was made easier by Spain's mounting domestic difficulties and her increasing willingness to accede to American demands, particularly after the accession of the Sagasta Ministry and the removal of Weyler. It was made more difficult by the public's increasing sympathy for Cuba and its growing hatred of Spain. It was made impossible by the high emotional pitch to which the public was raised following the destruction of the *Maine*. Responsibility for this state of mind rests primarily with the press.

In the opinion of the writer, the Spanish-American War would not have occurred had not the appearance of Hearst in New York journalism precipitated a bitter battle for newspaper circulation. The Cuban insurrection and its attendant horrors furnished a unique opportunity to the proprietors of the sensational press to prove their enterprise and provide the type of news that sold papers. Even the conservative journals, irritated by the emphasis the "new journalists" placed upon Cuba, were compelled by that very emphasis to devote considerably more space to Cuban affairs than they otherwise would have done.

In their treatment of Cuban affairs, none of the papers seemed primarily concerned with Cuba *per se,* with the possible exception of the *Sun,* on whose staff Martí had once been included, and the less important *Times.* Partisan newspapers, such as the *Tribune* and the *Mail and Express,* so critical of Cleveland's policy of non-intervention, were in complete accord with McKinley's similar stand. The *Evening Post's* principal concern in the Cuban matter was the maintenance of the highest standards of journalistic integrity and national honor. Thoroughly exasperated by the tactics of the pro-Cuban journals, Godkin was indeed impelled to lean backwards in his attempts to dispel the violent outbursts of Hearst, Pulitzer, and Dana. The *Journal of Commerce* saw in Cuba only a menace to peace and prosperity. The *Herald* was more concerned with maintaining peace with Spain than securing justice for Cuba. The *Journal* and *World* simply used Cuba to achieve their prime purpose — an increase in circulation. When one gained a scoop by furnishing some fresh proof of Spanish cruelty or Cuban suffering, the other was perfectly willing to injure the Cuban cause by depreciating the effort of its rival, or even by exploding the scoop, if it could: witness the Cisneros case and the *Olivette* "outrage."

The most widely circulated of the newspapers were the least honestly objective

in the reporting of news and in the presentation of editorial opinion. Reporters, aware of the policies of their papers, produced the type of news most acceptable to their editors. Hearst's famous reply to the artist Remington's complaint that there was no war in Cuba — "You furnish the pictures; I'll furnish the war," — well illustrates the degree of objectivity that prevailed. George Bronson Rea, *Herald* reporter during 1896–1898, who ruthlessly exposed many of Scovel's widely circulated atrocity stories, informed the writer that his friendship for Scovel was unimpaired by the incident, both recognizing the necessity of conforming to the policies of their papers. It is significant to note, with the advent of Hearst, that the rival *World* began to extol the virtues of its decidedly pro-Cuban reporter, Scovel, as it once had those of its more objective Bowen.

Upon the already biased reports from Cuba, the home offices of the newspapers built further. Artists far removed from the Cuban scene illustrated reports vividly but inaccurately; cartoonists magnified atrocities; feature writers, Sunday supplement writers, even contributors to women's pages added their prejudiced efforts. With so much information and misinformation from which to choose, editorial writers knew no bounds.

New York's newspapers set the standards of national journalism. The *World* was the leading Democratic organ in the country; the *Tribune,* one of the most important Republican sheets; the *Sun* was read by newspaper men throughout the nation, as was the *Post.* The *Journal's* sensational innovations won immediate national attention and some imitation. When New York's powerful newspapers emphasized Cuban news, it was natural that others should do the same.

From March, 1895, until April, 1898,

there were fewer than a score of days in which Cuba did not appear in the day's news. The newspaper reading public was subjected to a constantly increasing bombardment, the heaviest guns booming for "Cuba Libre." The effect was cumulative. The average reader, naturally sympathetic to the cause of freedom and critical of monarchies, became convinced that Spain was arrogant, insulting, vindictive, cruel, that Weyler and his cohorts were brutes in human form, that Cánovas was a relic of medieval intolerance; Muruaga and De Lome, blundering hypocrites; Sagasta and Blanco, weak nincompoops. So thoroughly convinced was the reader of the treachery of Spaniards that he naturally attributed the loss of the *Maine* to a deliberate act of Spain. So thoroughly convinced was he of Spanish guile and deceitfulness that he completely agreed when the newspapers brushed aside the Spanish promise to end hostilities, and public opinion compelled McKinley to do the same. Furthermore, the press had driven home the lesson that Spain was cowardly and weak, bankrupt, racked by internal dissension, friendless, and would prove no match for the magnificent forces of the United States: in short, that the "crusade for humanity" would prove little more than a picnic.

Little wonder that the "average reader," indoctrinated with these opinions, called on his Government for War.

Richard Hofstadter:
MANIFEST DESTINY AND THE PHILIPPINES

THE taking of the Philippine Islands from Spain in 1899 marked a major historical departure for the American people. It was a breach in their traditions and a shock to their established values. To be sure, from their national beginnings they had constantly engaged in expansion, but almost entirely into contiguous territory. Now they were extending themselves to distant extrahemispheric colonies; they were abandoning a strategy of defense hitherto limited to the continent and its appurtenances, in favor of a major strategic commitment in the Far East; and they were now supplementing the spread of a relatively homogeneous population into territories destined from the beginning for self-government with a far different procedure in which control was imposed by force on millions of ethnic aliens. The acquisition of the islands, therefore, was understood by contemporaries on both sides of the debate, as it is readily understood today, to be a turning-point in our history.

To discuss the debate in isolation from other events, however, would be to deprive it of its full significance. American entrance into the Philippine Islands was a by-product of the Spanish-American War. The Philippine crisis is inseparable from the war crisis, and the war crisis itself is inseparable from a larger constellation that might be called "the psychic crisis of the 1890's."

Central in the background of the psychic crisis was the great depression that broke in 1893 and was still very acute

Reprinted from *America in Crisis* by Daniel Aaron, ed., by permission of Alfred A. Knopf, Inc., copyright 1952, pp. 173–200.

when the agitation over the war in Cuba began. Severe depression, by itself, does not always generate an emotional crisis as intense as that of the nineties. In the 1870's the country had been swept by a depression of comparable acuteness and duration which, however, did not give rise to all the phenomena that appeared in the 1890's or to very many of them with comparable intensity and impact. It is often said that the 1890's, unlike the 1870's, form some kind of a "watershed" in American history. The difference between the emotional and intellectual impact of these two depressions can be measured, I believe, not by any difference in severity, but rather by reference to a number of singular events that in the 1890's converged with the depression to heighten its impact upon the public mind.

First in importance was the Populist movement, the free-silver agitation, the heated campaign of 1896. For the first time in our history a depression had created an allegedly "radical" movement strong enough to capture a major party and raise the specter, however unreal, of drastic social convulsion. Second was the maturation and bureaucratization of American business, the completion of its essential industrial plant, and the development of trusts on a scale sufficient to stir the anxiety that the old order of competitive opportunities was approaching an eclipse. Third, and of immense symbolic importance, was the apparent filling up of the continent and disappearance of the frontier line. We now know how much land had not yet been taken up and how great were the remaining possibilities of internal expansion both in business and on the land; but to the mind of the 1890's it seemed that the resource that had engaged the energies of the people for three centuries had been used up; the frightening possibility suggested itself that a serious juncture in the nation's history had come. As Frederick Jackson Turner expressed it in his famous paper of 1893: "Now, four centuries from the discovery of America, at the end of one hundred years of life under the Constitution, the frontier has gone, and with its going has closed the first period of American history."

To middle-class citizens who had been brought up to think in terms of the nineteenth-century order, things looked bad. Farmers in the staple-growing region seemed to have gone mad over silver and Bryan; workers were stirring in bloody struggles like the Homestead and Pullman strikes; the supply of new land seemed at an end; the trust threatened the spirit of business enterprise; civic corruption was at a high point in the large cities; great waves of seemingly unassimilable immigrants arrived yearly and settled in hideous slums. To many historically conscious writers, the nation seemed overripe, like an empire ready for collapse through a stroke from outside or through internal upheaval. Acute as the situation was for all those who lived by the symbols of national power — for the governing and thinking classes — it was especially poignant for young people, who would have to make their careers in the dark world that seemed to be emerging.

The symptomatology of the crisis might record several tendencies in popular thought and behavior that had not been observable before or had existed only in pale and tenuous form. These symptoms fall into two basic moods. The key to one of them is an intensification of protest and humanitarian reform. Populism, Utopianism, the rise of the Christian Social gospel, the growing intellectual interest in Socialism, the social settlement movement that appealed so strongly to the college generation of the nineties, the quickening of protest in the realistic novel — all of these are expressions of this mood. The other is one of national self-assertion, aggression, expansion. The tone of the first was sympathy, of the second, power. During the 1890's far more patriotic groups were founded than in any other decade of our history; the naval theories of Captain Mahan were gaining in influence; naval construction was booming; there was an immense quickening of the American cult of Napoleon and a vogue of the virile and martial writings of Rudyard Kipling; young Theodore Roosevelt became the exemplar of the vigorous, masterful, out-of-doors man; the revival of European imperialism stirred speculation over what America's place would be in the world of renewed colonial rivalries. But most significant was the rising tide of jingoism, a matter of constant comment among observers of American life during the decade.

Jingoism, of course, was not new in American history. But during the 1870's and '80's the American public had been notably quiescent about foreign relations. There had been expansionist statesmen, but they had been blocked by popular apathy and statecraft had been restrained. Grant had failed dismally in his attempt to acquire Santo Domingo; our policy toward troubled Hawaii had been cautious; in 1877 an offer of two Haitian naval harbors had been spurned. In responding to Haiti, Secretary of State Frelinghuysen had remarked that "the policy of this Government . . . has tended toward avoidance of possessions disconnected from the main continent."[1] Henry Cabot Lodge, in his life of George Washington published

in 1889, observed that foreign relations then filled "but a slight place in American politics, and excite generally only a languid interest." Within a few years this comment would have seemed absurd; the history of the 1890's is the history of public agitation over expansionist issues and of quarrels with other nations.

Three primary incidents fired American jingoism between the spring of 1891 and the close of 1895. First came Secretary of State Blaine's tart and provocative reply to the Italian minister's protest over the lynching of eleven Italians in New Orleans. Then there was friction with Chile over a riot in Valparaiso in which two American sailors were killed and several injured by a Chilean mob. In 1895 occurred the more famous Venezuela boundary dispute with Britain. Discussion of these incidents would take us too far afield, but note that they all had these characteristics in common: in none of them was national security or the national interest vitally involved; in all three American diplomacy was extraordinarily and disproportionately aggressive; in all three the possibility of war was contemplated; and in each case the American public and press response was enthusiastically nationalist.

It is hard to read the history of these events without concluding that politicians were persistently using jingoism to restore

---

[1] Albert K. Weinberg: *Manifest Destiny* (Baltimore: 1935), p. 252. There is a suggestive similarity to the conditions of the nineties in the circumstances attending the Cuban insurrection of 1868–78. The hostilities were even more bitter and exhausting than those of 1895–8; its latter phases also corresponded with an acute depression in the United States; the case of the *Virginius* offered a pretext for war almost as satisfactory as that of the *Maine*. Some public and press clamor followed. But it did not rise even near to the pitch of overwhelming pressure for war. Two things were supplied in the nineties that were missing in the seventies: a psychic crisis that generated an expansionist mood, and the techniques of yellow journalism. Cf. Samuel Flagg Bemis: *A Diplomatic History of the United States* (New York: 1936), pp. 433–5.

their prestige, mend their party fences, and divert the public mind from grave internal discontents. It hardly seems an accident that jingoism and Populism rose together. Documentary evidence for the political exploitation of foreign crises is not overwhelmingly abundant, in part because such a motive is not necessarily conscious and where it is conscious it is not likely to be confessed or recorded. The persistence of jingoism in every administration from Harrison's to Theodore Roosevelt's, however, is too suggestive to be ignored. During the nineties the press of each party was fond of accusing the other of exploiting foreign conflict. We know that Blaine was not above twisting the British lion's tail for political purposes; and there is no reason to believe that he would have exempted Italy from the same treatment. We know too that Harrison, on the eve of the Chile affair, for the acuteness of which he was primarily responsible, was being urged by prominent Republican politicians who had the coming Presidential campaign in mind to pursue a more aggressive foreign policy because it would "have the . . . effect of diverting attention from stagnant political discussions." And although some Democratic papers charged that he was planning to run for re-election during hostilities so that he could use the "don't-swap-horses-in-the-middle-of-the-stream" appeal, many Democrats felt that it was politically necessary for them to back him against Chile so that, as one of their Congressmen remarked, the Republicans could not "run away with all the capital there is to be made in an attempt to assert national self-respect." Grover Cleveland admittedly was a man of exceptional integrity whose stand against pressure for the annexation of Hawaii during 1893-4 does him much credit. But precisely for this act of abnegation his administration

fell under the charge made by Republican jingoes like Lodge and by many in his own party that he was indifferent to America's position in the world. And if Cleveland was too high-minded a man to exploit a needless foreign crisis, his Secretary of State, Richard Olney, was not. The Venezuela affair, which came at a very low point in the prestige of Cleveland's administration, offered Olney a rich chance to prove to critics in both parties that the administration was, after all, capable of vigorous diplomacy. That the crisis might have partisan value was not unthinkable to members of Olney's party. He received a suggestive letter from a Texas Congressman encouraging him to "go ahead," on the ground that the Venezuela issue was a "winner" in every section of the country. "When you come to diagnose the country's internal ills," his correspondent continued, "the possibilities of 'blood and iron' loom up immediately. Why, Mr. Secretary, just think of how angry the anarchistic, socialistic, and populistic boil appears on our political surface and who knows how deep its roots extend or ramify? One cannon shot across the bow of a British boat in defense of this principle will knock more *pus* out of it than would suffice to inoculate and corrupt our people for the next two centuries."

This pattern had been well established when the Cuban crisis broke out anew in 1895. It was quite in keeping that Secretary Olney should get a letter during the 1896 campaign from Fitzhugh Lee, the American consul in Havana, advising that the conservative faction of Gold Democrats become identified with the strong policy of mediation or intervention in Cuba. Thus, he argued, "the 'Sound Democrats' would get, with the Executive, the credit of stopping the wholesale atrocities daily practised here, the acquisition of Cuba by purchase, or by fighting a successful war, if war there be. In the latter case, the enthusiasm, the applications for service, the employment of many of the unemployed, might do much towards directing the minds of the people from imaginary ills, the relief of which is erroneously supposed to be reached by 'Free Silver'."

When President McKinley took office he was well aware that nationalist enthusiasm had reached a pitch that made war very likely. A few months earlier, he had told Senator Lodge that he might be "obliged" to go to war as soon as he entered the Presidency, and had expressed a preference that the Cuban crisis be settled one way or another in the time between his election and inauguration. Although he promised Carl Schurz that there would be "no jingo nonsense under my administration," he proved to have not quite enough strength to resist the current. Members of his own party put a great deal of pressure on him to give the people their war rather than endanger the Republican position. It was held that if war was inevitable, as presumably it was, it would be better for the President to lead than to be pushed; that resistance to war would be ruinous to the party; that going to war would prevent the Democrats from entering the next Presidential campaign with "Free Cuba" and "Free Silver" as their battle cries. After Senator Proctor's speech exposing conditions in Cuba the Chicago *Times-Herald,* a McKinley paper, declared that intervention in Cuba, peaceful or forcible, was "immediately inevitable. Our own internal political condition will not permit its postponement. . . . Let President McKinley hesitate to rise to the just expectation of the American people, and who can doubt that 'war for Cuban liberty' will be the crown of thorns that Free Silver

Democrats and Populists will adopt at the elections this fall. . . . The President would be powerless to stay any legislation, however ruinous to every sober, honest interest of the country." At the time McKinley sent his war message to Congress he knew quite well, and indeed made a passing reference to the fact, that Spain had already capitulated to the demands the United States had made upon her. This capitulation *could* have been made the basis of a peace message; instead it occupied one sentence tucked away near the end of a war message — a sentence that everyone chose to ignore. Evidently McKinley had concluded that what was wanted in the United States was not so much the freedom of Cuba as a *war* for the freedom of Cuba.

Historians say that the war was brought on by sensational newspapers. The press, spurred by the rivalry between Pulitzer and Hearst, aroused sympathy with the Cubans and hatred of Spain and catered to the bellicosity of the public. No one seems to have asked: *Why was the public so fatally receptive to war propaganda?* I believe the answer must be sought in the causes of the jingoism that had raged for seven years before the war actually broke out. The events of the nineties had brought frustration and anxiety to civically conscious Americans. On one hand, as Mark Sullivan has commented, the American during this period was disposed "to see himself as an underdog in economic situations and controversies in his own country"; but the civic frustrations of the era created also a restless aggressiveness, a desire to be assured that the power and vitality of the nation were not waning. The capacity for sympathy and the need for power existed side by side. That highly typical and symptomatic American, William Allen White, recalls in his *Autobiography* how during the nineties he was "bound to my idols — Whitman, the great democrat, and Kipling, the imperialist." In varying stages of solution the democrat and imperialist existed in the hearts of White's countrymen — the democrat disposed to free Cuba, the imperialist to vent his civic spleen on Spain.

I suspect that the readiness of the public to over-react to the Cuban situation can be understood in part through the displacement of feelings of sympathy or social protest generated in domestic affairs; these impulses found a safe and satisfactory discharge in foreign conflict. Spain was portrayed in the press as waging a heartless and inhuman war; the Cubans were portrayed as noble victims of Spanish tyranny, their situation as analogous to that of Americans in 1776. When one examines the sectional and political elements that were most enthusiastic about the war, one finds them not primarily among the wealthy Eastern big-business Republicans who supported McKinley and read the conservative dignified newspapers, but in the Bryan sections of the country, in the *Democratic Party*, and among the patrons of the yellow journals. During the controversy significant charges were hurled back and forth; conservative peace-advocates claimed that many jingoists were hoping for a costly war over Cuba that could be made the occasion of a return to free silver; in return, the inflammatory press often fell into the pattern of Populist rhetoric, declaiming, for example, about "the eminently respectable porcine citizens who — for dollars in the money-grubbing sty, support 'conservative' newspapers and consider the starvation of . . . inoffensive men, women and children, and the murder of 250 American sailors . . . of less importance than a fall of two points in a price of stocks." Although imputations

of base economic motives were made by both sides, it is also significant that the current of sympathy and agitation ran strong where a discontented constituency, politically frustrated by Bryan's defeat, was most numerous. An opportunity to discharge aggressions against "Wall Street interests" cooly indifferent to the fate of both Cuban *insurrectos* and staple farmers may have been more important than the more rationalized and abstract linkage between a war and free silver. The primary significance of the war for the psychic economy of the nineties was that it served as an outlet for aggressive impulses while presenting itself, quite truthfully, as an idealistic and humanitarian crusade. The American public was not interested in the material gains of an intervention in Cuba. It never dreamed that the war would lead to the taking of the Philippines. Starting a war for a high-minded and altruistic purpose and then transmuting it into a war for annexation was unthinkable; it would be, as McKinley put it in a phrase that later came back to haunt him, "criminal aggression."

There is one odd paradox in the evolution of sentiment from a war over freeing Cuba to a peace treaty acquiring the Philippines by conquest. The big-business - conservative - Republican-McKinley element, overwhelmingly hostile to this romantic and sentimental war, quickly became interested in the imperialism that grew out of it. The popular Populist-Democratic-Bryanite element, which had been so keen for the war, became the stronghold — although by no means resolute or unbroken — of opposition to the fruits of war. This much, however, must be said of both the populace and the business community: if the matter had been left either to public clamor or to business interests, there would have been no American entrance into the Philippines in 1898.

The dynamic element in the movement for imperialism was a small group of politicians, intellectuals, and publicists, including Senator Henry Cabot Lodge, Theodore Roosevelt, John Hay, Senator Albert J. Beveridge, Whitelaw Reid, editor of the *New York Tribune*, Albert Shaw, editor of the *Review of Reviews*, Walter Hines Page, editor of the *Atlantic Monthly*, and Henry and Brooks Adams.

Most of these men came from what are known as good families. They were well educated, cultivated, patrician in outlook, Anglo-Saxon in background, noncommercial in personal goals and standards, and conservative reformers in politics. Although living in a commercial world, they could not accept business standards for their own careers nor absorb themselves into the business community. Although they lived in a vulgar democracy, they were not democratic by instinct. They could not and did not care to succeed in politics of the corrupt sort that had become so common in America. They had tried their hands at civic reform, had found it futile, and had become bored with it. When they did not, like Henry Adams, turn away from American life in bitterness, they became interested in some large and statesmanlike theater of action, broader than American domestic policy. Although there were men of this sort in the Democratic ranks, like Walter Hines Page, they were most influential within the Republican Party, which during the mid-nineties had become committed to a policy of expansion.

In general, this group of imperialists was inspired by the navalist theories of Mahan and by the practical example of what they sometimes referred to as Mother England. They saw that a new phase of imperialism had opened in the Western world at large, and they were fearful that if the United States did not adopt a policy of expansion and preparation for military and naval struggle, it would be left behind in what they referred to as the struggle for life or, at other times, as the march of the nations. They were much concerned that the United States expand its army and particularly its navy; that it dig an isthmian canal; that it acquire the naval bases and colonies in the Caribbean and the Pacific necessary to protect such a canal; that it annex Hawaii and Samoa. At their most aggressive, they also called for the annexation of Canada, and the expulsion of European powers from the Western hemisphere. They were much interested in the Far East as a new theater of political conflict and investment possibilities. They were, indeed, more interested than business itself in the Pacific area, particularly in China, as a potential market. As Professor Pratt has observed: "The need of American business for colonial markets and fields for investment was discovered not by businessmen but by historians and other intellectuals, by journalists and politicians."

The central figure in this group was Theodore Roosevelt, who more than any other single man was responsible for our entry into the Philippines. Throughout the 1890's Roosevelt had been eager for a war, whether it be with Chile, Spain, or England. A war with Spain, he felt, would get us "a proper navy and a good system of coast defenses," would free Cuba from Spain, and would help to free America from European domination, would give "our people . . . something to think of that isn't material gain," and would try "both the army and navy in actual practice." Roosevelt feared that the United States would grow heedless of its defense, take insufficient care to develop its power, and become "an easy prey for any people which still retained those most valuable of all qualities, the soldierly virtues." "All the great masterful races have been fighting races," he argued. There were higher virtues than those of peace and material comfort. "No triumph of peace is quite so great as the supreme triumphs of war." Such was the philosophy of the man who secured Commodore Dewey's appointment to the Far Eastern Squadron and alerted him before the actual outbreak of hostilities to be prepared to engage the Spanish fleet at Manila.

Our first step into the Philippines presented itself to us as a "defensive" measure. Dewey's attack on the Spanish fleet in Manila Bay was made on the assumption that the Spanish fleet, if unmolested, might cross the Pacific and bombard the West Coast cities of the United States. I do not know whether American officialdom was aware that this fleet was so decrepit that it could hardly have gasped its way across the ocean. Next, Dewey's fleet seemed in danger unless its security were underwritten by the dispatch of American troops to Manila. To be sure, having accomplished his mission, Dewey could have removed this "danger" simply by leaving Manila Bay. However, in war one is always tempted to hold whatever gains have been made, and at Dewey's request American troops were dispatched very promptly after the victory and arrived at Manila in July 1898. Thus our second step into the Philippines was again a "defensive" measure. The third step was the so-called "capture" of Manila, which was actually carried out in cooperation with the Spaniards, who were allowed to make a token resistance, and in exclusion of the Filipino patriots under Aguinaldo. The fourth step was an agreement, incorporated in the protocol suspending hostilities between the United States and Spain, that the United States would occupy the city, bay, and harbor of Manila pending a final settlement in the peace treaty. The fifth step came much later, on December 21, 1898, when McKinley instructed the War Department to extend the military government already in force at Manila to the entire archipelago. This began a fierce revolt by the Filipino patriots, who felt that they had been led to expect a much different policy from the American government. Two days before the vote was taken in the Senate on the ratification of the peace treaty, the patriots and the American forces fought their first battle and American soldiers were killed, a fact that seems to have had an important influence on public discussion. Once again, administrative action had given a sharp bias to the whole process of political decision. Tyler Dennett goes so far as to say that by authorizing a campaign of conquest while the Senate was still discussing the situation, McKinley "created a situation . . . which had the, effect of coercing the Senate." This is a doubtful conclusion, but there is some reason to believe that the hand of expansionists was strengthened by the feeling that opposition to the administration's policy would be unpatriotic.

This much can certainly be said: by the time our policy could be affected by public discussion a great deal had already been accomplished by the annexationists. The tone of the argument was already weighted towards staying in simply because we were there. As McKinley put it: "It is not a question of keeping the islands of the East, but of leaving them." It is not an easy thing to persuade a people or a government during the pitch of war enthusiasm to abandon a potential gain already in hand. Moreover, a great social interest hitherto indifferent to the Philippines, the business community, quickly swung around to an expansionist position. The Protestant clergy, seeing a potential enlargement of missionary enterprise, also threw in its weight. For the first time the group of imperialists and navalists had powerful allies. Business began to talk about the Philippines as a possible gateway to the markets of eastern Asia, the potentialities of which were thought to be very large. The little imperialist group was much heartened and, with the help of Navy officers, put increasing pressure upon a rather hesitant administration to follow through.

There seemed four possible ways of disposing of the Philippine problem. The first, returning the islands to Spain, found favor nowhere. The second, selling or otherwise alienating the Philippines to some other power, seemed to invite a possible general European war; and it would hardly be more justified morally than remaining in possession ourselves. Moreover, we were being encouraged by England to remain in the Philippines, for American possession of those islands was much more palatable to England than possession by any other power. The third possibility, leaving the Philippines to themselves and giving them the independence Aguinaldo's men had been fighting for, was equivalent in most American minds to leaving them to anarchy. It also seemed to be another way of encouraging a scramble among other powers interested in the Far East. The final possibility was some form of American possession, in the form of a protectorate or otherwise. In the beginning there was much sentiment for merely retaining a naval base and coaling station on the island of Luzon, or perhaps the island of Luzon itself. Second thought suggested, however, that such a base would be endangered if the rest of the islands were left open to possible occupation by other nations. The dynamics of the situation suggested an all-or-none policy, and the administration drifted rapidly towards annexation of the entire archipelago.

The American public had not previously been either informed about or interested in the Philippines. In the entire eighty-year period from 1818 through May 1898, only thirty-five articles about the islands had appeared in American magazines. At the moment of Dewey's victory the press, although given over to encouraging the public jubilation, did not show an immediate interest in taking the islands. However, sentiment grew with considerable rapidity. As early as July 1898, the *Literary Digest* noted that the leading Republican papers were pro-expansion. A sample of 65 newspapers taken by the magazine *Public Opinion* in August showed that 43 per cent were for permanent retention of the Philippines, 24.6 per cent were opposed, and 32.4 per cent were wavering. In this case, "wavering" usually meant formerly opposed to expansion but apparently changing views. By December 1898, when the crucial debate in the Senate was beginning, the *New York Herald* polled 498 newspapers on the subject of expansion and found that 305, or 61.3 per cent, were favorable. New England and the Middle States showed clear margins in favor of expansion, the West an overwhelming margin; the South alone, by a thin margin, was opposed. The state of press opinion does not *measure* public feeling, but probably does indicate the direction in which public opinion was moving.

To President McKinley, a benign and far from aggressive man, public sentiment was of great importance. He was not a man to lead the American people in a direction in which their sympathies were not already clearly bent. There was a current joke: "Why is McKinley's mind like a bed? Because it has to be made up for him every time he wants to use it." However unjust to the President, this does characterize his response to public opinion. He was not by temperament an expansionist, but if his immediate advisers and the public at large were preponderantly for annexation, he was willing to go along, and was thoroughly capable of finding good reasons for doing so. During the fall of 1898 he left Washington for a tour of the West, and made a great many brief speeches sounding out public opinion on annexation of the Philippines, on which he seems to have tentatively been determined in his own mind. He found a warm reception for himself and an enthusiastic response to the idea of expansion. Evidently his intent was confirmed by this exposure to public opinion and also by advices concerning the state of the public mind from correspondents and advisers, and when he returned to Washington those who were opposed to expansion found him unmovable. The Peace Commission negotiating the treaty in Paris was instructed to ask for all the Philippine Islands, and this provision was included in the peace treaty signed on December 10, 1898.

The debate over the retention of the Philippines then went through two phases. During the first, which lasted from December 1898 to the second week in February 1899, the question was argued both in the Senate and in the forums of public opinion. This phase neared its end when, on February 6, the Senate narrowly voted to ratify the peace treaty; it was definitively closed on February 14, when a resolution sponsored by Senator Bacon of Georgia, calling for early Philippine independence, was rejected by the preciously narrow margin of one vote — the casting vote of the Vice President, which resolved a 29-29 tie. The

second phase of the debate extended throughout 1899 and 1900, when American policy toward the Philippines was a matter of general public discussion and a partisan issue in the Presidential campaign of 1900.

Who was for and who against annexation? In large measure it was a party issue. The *New York Herald* poll showed that of 241 Republican papers 84.2 per cent were *for* expansion, and of 174 Democratic papers 71.3 per cent were *against* expansion. In some degree it was also a young man's movement. Geographically it extended throughout all sections of the country, and seems to have been favored everywhere but in the South, although even there it was strong. We do not have a clear index of public opinion for the period, but the practical politicians, whose business it was to gauge public sentiment in the best way they knew, concluded that the preponderant feeling was overwhelmingly for annexation.

The debate over the acquisition of the Philippines was perhaps no more than a ceremonial assertion of the values of both sides. The real decisions were made in the office of Theodore Roosevelt, in the Senate cloakroom, in the sanctums of those naval officers from whom the McKinley administration got its primary information about the Philippines during its period of doubt over annexation, and, by McKinley's own testimony, in the privacy of his chambers late at night. The public was, by and large, faced with a *fait accompli* that, although theoretically reversible, had the initial impetus of its very existence to carry it along. The intensity of the public discussion, at any rate, showed that the American conscience had really been shocked. No type of argument was neglected on either side. Those who wanted to take the Philippines pointed to the potential markets of the

East, the White Man's Burden, the struggle for existence, "racial" destiny, American traditions of expansion, the dangers of a general war if the Philippines were left open to a European scramble, the almost parental duty of assuming responsibility for the allegedly child-like Filipinos, the incapacity of the Filipinos for self-government, and so on. The anti-imperialists based their essential appeal on political principle. They pointed out that the United States had come into existence pledged to the idea that man should not be governed without his consent. They suggested that the violation of these political traditions (under which the nation had prospered) was not only a gross injustice to others, of which we should feel deeply ashamed, but also a way of tempting Providence and risking degeneration and disintegration as a sort of punishment for the atrophy of one's own principles. They pointed also to the expense of overseas dominions, standing armies and navalism, and the danger of being embroiled in imperialist wars.

Many leading anti-imperialists were men of great distinction; their ranks included by far the greater part of the eminent figures of the literary and intellectual world. Most of them were, however, in the unfortunate position of opposing the fruits of a war that they had either favored or failed to oppose. Unlike the expansionists, they did not have complete control of a major party (there were more expansionists among the Democrats than there were anti-expansionists among the Republicans). They were hopelessly heterogeneous: Gold Democrats, Bryan Democrats, New-England-conscience Republicans, and a scattering of reformers and intellectuals.

They organized late — the Anti-Imperialist League grew up in the months after November 1898 — and their political leadership, however ardent in sentiment, pursued a hesitant and uncertain course. Their most eminent political leaders were chiefly old men, and the strongest appeal of the anti-imperialist movement seems to have been to the old, high-principled elements in the country, while the imagination of the young was fired far more by the rhetoric of expansionism. It seems clear that the main chance of this minority was to use its position in the Senate to deny the necessary two-thirds approval to the peace treaty acquiring the islands from Spain. Here the opponents of annexation might have delayed it long enough to give themselves a chance to reach the public. But William Jennings Bryan, for reasons that are not altogether clear, persuaded enough members of his party to vote for the treaty to lose the case. Bryan hoped to continue the fight, of course, and grant independence later, but over his conduct and his explanations there hangs a heavy sense of inevitable defeat, stemming from his recognition that the voice of the majority demanded the bold and aggressive policy.

In the arguments for annexation two essential moral and psychological themes appeared over and over again. These themes were expressed in the words Duty and Destiny. According to the first, to reject annexation of the Philippines would be to fail of fulfilling a solemn obligation. According to the second, annexation of the Philippines in particular, and expansion generally, were inevitable and irresistible.

The people had entered the war for what they felt to be purely altruistic and humanitarian reasons — the relief and liberation of the Cubans. The idea that territorial gains should arise out of this pure-hearted war of liberation, and the fact that before long the Americans stood in the same relation to the Filipinos as the Spaniards had stood to the Cubans, was most uncomfortable. These things raised moral questions that the anti-imperialists did not neglect to express and exploit. The imperialists were accused of breaking our national word, of violating the pledge made by McKinley himself that by our moral code forcible annexation would be "criminal aggression." They were also accused of violating the solemn injunctions of the Founding Fathers, particularly the principles of the Declaration of Independence. The rhetoric of Duty was a reassuring answer to this attempt to stir feelings of guilt.

The feeling that one may be guilty of wrongdoing can be heightened when the questionable act is followed by adversity. Conversely, it may be minimized by the successful execution of a venture. Misfortune is construed as providential punishment; but success, as in the Calvinist scheme, is taken as an outward sign of an inward state of grace. One of the most conspicuous things about the war was the remarkable successes achieved by American arms, of which the most astonishing was Dewey's destruction, without losing a single American life, of the entire Spanish Eastern fleet in Manila Bay. Victories of this sort could readily be interpreted as Providential signs, tokens of Divine approval. It was widely reported in the United States that this was Dewey's own interpretation. "If I were a religious man, and I hope I am," he said, "I should say that the hand of God was in it." This was precisely the sort of reassurance that was needed. "The magnificent fleets of Spain," declared a writer in a Baptist periodical, concerning Spain's senile and decrepit navy, "have gone down as marvelously, I had almost said, as miraculously, as the walls of Jericho went down." The victory, said an editor of the *Christian and Missionary Alliance,* "read almost like the

stories of the ancient battles of the Lord in the times of Joshua, David, and Jehoshophat."

Furthermore, what might have seemed a sin became transformed into a positive obligation, a duty. The feeling was: *Providence has been so indulgent to us, by giving us so richly of success, that we would be sinful if we did not accept the responsibility it has asked us to assume.* The Protestant clergy, those tender guardians of the national conscience, did not hesitate to make lavish use of such arguments. "To give to the world the life more abundant both for here and hereafter," reasoned a writer in the *Baptist Missionary Review,* "is the duty of the American people by virtue of the call of God. This call is very plain. The hand of God in history has ever been plain." "If God has brought us to the parting of the ways," insisted a writer in the *Churchman,* "we cannot hold back without rejecting divine leadership." The rhetoric of secular leaders was hardly less inspired. "We will not renounce our part in the mission of our race, trustees under God, of the civilization of the world," said Senator Albert J. Beveridge. "God has not been preparing the English-speaking and Teutonic peoples for a thousand years for nothing but vain and idle self-contemplation and self-admiration. No! He has made us the master organizers of the world to establish system where chaos reigns. He has made us adepts in government that we may administer government among savages and senile peoples."

The theme of Destiny was a corollary of the theme of Duty. Repeatedly it was declared that expansion was the result of a "cosmic tendency," that "destiny always arrives," that it was in the "inexorable logic of events," and so on. The doctrine that expansion was inevitable had of course long been familiar to Americans;

we all know how often Manifest Destiny was invoked throughout the nineteenth century. Albert Weinberg has pointed out, however, that this expression took on a new meaning in the nineties. Previously destiny had meant primarily that American expansion, *when we willed it,* could not be resisted *by others* who might wish to stand in our way. During the nineties it came to mean that expansion "could not be resisted by Americans themselves, caught, willing or unwilling," in the coils of fate. A certain reluctance on our part was implied. This was not quite so much what we *wanted* to do; it was what we *had* to do. Our aggression was implicitly defined as compulsive — the product not of our own wills but of objective necessity (or the will of God).

"Duty," said President McKinley, "determines destiny." While Duty meant that we had a moral obligation, Destiny meant that we would certainly fulfill it, that the capacity to fulfill it was inherent in us. Our history had been a continuous history of expansion; it had always succeeded before, therefore it was certain to succeed in the future. Expansion was a national and "racial" inheritance, a deep and irresistible inner necessity. Here was a plausible traditionalist answer to the accusation of a grave breach of tradition.

It is not surprising that the public should have found some truth in this concept of inevitable destiny, for the acts that first involved their country with the fate of the Philippines were willed and carried out by others and were made objects for public discussion and decision only *after* the most important commitments had been made. The public will was not freely exercised upon the question, and for the citizens at large, who were in the presence of forces they could not understand or control, the rhetoric of Destiny may have been a way of softening and ennobling the *fait accompli* with which they were presented. But what of the men whose wills were really effective in the matter? If we examine their case, we find that the manufacturers of inevitability believed deeply in their own product. Indeed, while the extent to which the idea of Destiny was generally accepted is unknown, its wide prevalence among influential politicians, editors, and publicists is beyond argument. When Senator Lodge wrote to Theodore Roosevelt in 1898 that "the whole policy of annexation is growing rapidly under the irresistible pressure of events," when President McKinley remarked in private to his secretary, concerning the taking of Hawaii, "It is manifest destiny," when he declared in his private instructions to the peace commissioners that "the march of events rules and overrules human action" — what was involved was not an attempt to sell an idea to the public but a mode of communication in which the insiders felt thoroughly at home; perhaps a magical mode of thought by which they quieted their own uncertainties. It is easy to say, from the perspective of the twentieth century, that where contemporaries heard the voice of God we think we can discern the carnal larynx of Theodore Roosevelt. But if the insiders themselves imagined that they heard the voice of God, we must be careful of imputing hypocrisy. It is significant that the idea of Destiny was effective even among people who had very grave doubts about the desirability of remaining in the Philippines. Secretary of the Navy John D. Long, who was affectionately regarded by Theodore Roosevelt as an old fuddy-duddy on this score, confided to a friend in 1898 that he would really have preferred the United States to remain what it had been during the first half of the nineteenth century — "provincial," as he expressed it, and "dominated by the New England idea. But," he added, "I cannot shut my eyes to the march of events — a march which seems to be beyond human control."

It would be false to give the impression that only high moral and metaphysical concepts were employed in the imperialistic argument. Talk about entry into the markets of Asia was heard often after Dewey's victory; but even those who talked about material gains showed a conspicuous and symptomatic inability to distinguish between interests, rights, and duties. Charles Denby, former minister to China and a member of McKinley's commission to study the Philippines, contributed to the *Forum* two interesting articles full of this confusion. The central business of diplomacy, confessed Denby, was to advance commerce. Our right to hold the Philippines was the right of conquerors. So far, Mr. Denby was all *Realpolitik*. But he continued that he favored keeping the islands because he could not conceive any alternative to doing so except seizing territory in China, and he did not want to oppress further "the helpless Government and people of China"! Thus a rather odd scruple crept in; but Mr. Denby quickly explained that this was simply because China's strength and prosperity were in America's interest. "We are after markets," he went on, sliding back into *Realpolitik*, and "along with these markets" — sliding back into morality — "will go our beneficent institutions; and humanity will bless us." In a second article Mr. Denby shuttled back to "the cold, hard practical question. . . . Will the possession of these islands benefit us as a nation? If it will not, set them free tomorrow, and let their people, if they please, cut each other's throats." And yet, Mr.

Denby made it clear, we did come as benefactors, bringing to our cut-throat friends "the choicest gifts — liberty and hope and happiness."

There was, besides the oscillatory rhetoric of Mr. Denby, a let's-be-candid school, whose views were expressed by the Washington *Post*: "All this talk about benevolent assimilation; all this hypocritical pretense of anxiety for the moral, social, and intellectual exaltation of the natives . . . deceives nobody, avails nothing. . . . We all know, down in our hearts, that these islands . . . are important to us only in the ratio of their practical possibilities, and by no other. . . . Why not be honest?"

There were others who found the primary benefit of our new imperial status in the social cohesion and military spirit that would result, hoping that the energies of the country would be deflected from internal to external conflict. "Marse" Henry Watterson, the well-known editor of the Louisville *Courier-Journal*, told a New York reporter: "From a nation of shopkeepers we become a nation of warriors. We escape the menace and peril of socialism and agrarianism, as England has escaped them, by a policy of colonization and conquest. From a provincial huddle of petty sovereignties held together by a rope of sand we rise to the dignity and prowess of an imperial republic incomparably greater than Rome. It is true that we exchange domestic dangers for foreign dangers; but in every direction we multiply the opportunities of the people. We risk Caesarism, certainly; but even Caesarism is preferable to anarchism. We risk wars; but a man has but one time to die, and either in peace or war, he is not likely to die until his time comes. . . . In short, *anything is better than the pace we were going be-*

fore these present forces were started into life. Already the young manhood of the country is as a goodly brand snatched from the burning, and given a perspective replete with noble deeds and elevating ideas."

Since Julius W. Pratt published his *Expansionists of 1898* fifteen years ago it has been obvious that any interpretation of America's entry upon the paths of imperialism in the nineties in terms of rational economic motives would not fit the facts, and that a historian who approached the event with preconceptions no more supple than those, say, of Lenin's *Imperialism* would be helpless. This is not to say that markets and investments have no bearing; they do, but there are innumerable features of the situation that they do not explain at all. In so far as the economic factor was important, it can be better studied in terms of the relation between the depression and the public mood.

The alternative explanation has been the equally simple idea that the war was a newpapers' war. This notion, once again, has some point, but it certainly does not explain the war itself, much less its expansionist result. The New Deal period showed that the press is not powerful enough to impose upon the public mind a totally uncongenial view of public events. It must operate roughly within the framework of public predispositions. Moreover, not all the papers of the nineties were yellow journals. We must inquire into the structure of journalistic power and also into the personnel of its ownership and editorship to find out what differentiated the sensational editors and publishers from those of the conservative press, and what it was about their readership that led the former to the (correct) conclusion that they could expand their circulations by resorting to jingo sensationalism.

There is still another qualification that must be placed upon the role of the press: the press itself, whatever it can do with opinion, does not have the power to precipitate opinion into action. That is something that takes place within the *political* process, and we cannot tell that part of the story without examining the state of party rivalries, the derivation and goals of the political elites, and indeed the entire political context. We must then supplement our story about the role of the newspapers with at least two other factors: the state of the public temper upon which the newspapers worked, and the manner in which party rivalries deflected domestic clashes into foreign aggression.

When we examine the public temper, we will find that the depression, together with such other events as the approaching completion of continental settlement, the growth of trusts, and the intensification of internal social conflict, had brought to large numbers of people intense frustrations in their economic lives and their careers. To others they had brought anxiety that a period of stagnation in national wealth and power had set in. The restlessness of the frustrated classes had been heightened by the defeat of Bryan in 1896. The anxieties about the national position had been increased among statesmen and publicists by the revival of world imperialism, in particular by the feeling that the nation was threatened by the aims of Germany, Russia, and Japan. The expansionist statesmen themselves were largely drawn from a restless upper-middle-class elite that had been fighting an unrewarding battle for conservative reform in domestic politics and that looked with some eagerness toward a more spacious field of action.

It is a psychological commonplace that we tend to respond to frustration with acts of aggression, and to allay anxieties by threatening acts against others. It seems suggestive that the underdog elements in Americans society showed a considerably higher responsiveness to the idea of war with Spain than the groups that were more satisfied with their economic or political positions. Our entry into the Philippines then aroused the interest of conservative groups that had been indifferent to the quixotism of freeing Cuba but were alert to the idea of capturing new markets. Imperialism appealed to members of both the business and political elites as an enlargement of the sphere of American power and profits. Many of the underdog elements also responded to this new note of national self-assertion; others, however, looked upon our conduct in the Philippines as a betrayal of national principles. Anti-expansionists attempted to stir a sense of guilt and foreboding in the nation at large. But the circumstances of the period 1898–1900 — the return of prosperity and the quick spectacular victories in war — made it difficult for them to impress this feeling upon the majority. The rhetoric of Duty and Destiny carried the day. The anti-expansionists had neither the numbers nor the morale of their opponents. The most conspicuous result of their lack of drive and confidence can be seen in the lamentable strategy of Bryan over the ratification of the treaty.

Clearly this attempt to see the war and expansion in the light of social history has led us onto the high and dangerous ground of social psychology. On this terrain we historians are at a great disadvantage; we are inexpert psychologists, and in any event we cannot get the kind of data for this period which would satisfactorily substantiate any psychological hypotheses. However, we have little other choice than to move into this terrain wherever simple rationalistic explanations of national behavior leave us dissatisfied. What I have attempted here is merely a preliminary sketch of a possible explanatory model that would enlarge our conception of our task. It needs further inquiry — which might make it seem more plausible at some points, more questionable at others.

A further warning is necessary: this study has been narrowly focused on a single incident. No effort has been made — and an effort should be made — to compare this crisis with other expansionist crises in our own history, which I suspect will show important differences. No effort has been made to compare American imperialism with that of other countries. No claim has been made either that the various features of our behavior are unique to our own country or that they are the same as those which will be found elsewhere. Many parallels can be found in the history of other nations to the role of the press and the parties in whipping up foreign crises. Parallels without number could be found to the role of the administration in largely committing the nation to a foreign policy before it could be made a matter of public discussion. The rhetoric and ideology of expansion also were not singular to us; duty, destiny, racism, and the other shibboleths can be found elsewhere. Only a careful comparative inquiry will tell us how our behavior in this situation compares with other instances of our own behavior, or with the behavior of other peoples in roughly comparable situations.

I cannot refrain from adding to these notes on the methods of historical understanding another note on the tragicomical procedure of history itself. It may be of some value to us to be reminded how some of the more grandiose expectations of the nineties were realized. Cuba, to be sure, which could have been freed in peace, was freed in the war — in so far as the little country of Batistas and Machados can be considered free. The sensational newspapers that had boomed the war lost money on expensive extras, costly war-news coverage, and declining advertising. I do not know whether those silverites who wanted the war really expected that it would remonetize silver, but if they did they were rewarded with McKinley's renewed triumph and the Gold Standard Act of 1900. As for business, the gigantic markets of the East never materialized, and the precise value of the Philippines in getting at them is arguable. The islands themselves proved to be a mildly profitable colony that came to absorb a little over one per cent of all United States investments abroad. Yet within a generation the United States had committed itself to restoring independence to the Philippines. When this promise was enacted in 1934 many descendants of Aguinaldo's rebels were unenthusiastic about their new economic and strategic position. Finally, the exact estimation that is to be put on our strategic commitment in the Far East, which began with the Philippines, is still a matter of debate. We should, however, make note of the earlier opinion of one of our most brilliant and farsighted statesmen, who declared in 1907 that the Philippines were the Achilles' heel of our strategic position and should be given "nearly complete independence" at the "earliest possible moment." The author of these remarks was Theodore Roosevelt.

Henry Cabot Lodge: THE PHILIPPINE ISLANDS

A SPEECH BEFORE THE UNITED STATES SENATE, MARCH 7, 1900

THE policy we offer is simple and straightforward. We believe in the frank acceptance of existing facts, and in dealing with them as they are and not on a theory of what they might or ought to be. We accept the fact that the Philippine Islands are ours to-day and that we are responsible for them before the world. The next fact is that there is a war in those islands. Our immediate duty, therefore, is to suppress this disorder, put an end to fighting, and restore peace and order. That is what we are doing. Further than the acts and the policy which I have just stated, I can only give my own opinion and belief as to the future, and as to the course to be pursued in the Philippines.

I hope and believe that we shall retain the islands, and that, peace and order once restored, we shall and should reestablish civil government, beginning with the towns and villages, where the inhabitants are able to manage their own affairs. We should give them honest administration, and prompt and efficient courts. We should see to it that there is entire protection to persons and property,

From *The Congressional Record*, 60th Congress, 1st Session, Volume 33, Part 3, pp. 2618–2630. NOTE: Only essential parts of this speech are reproduced here. No attempt has been made to indicate parts omitted or to retain the paragraphing of the original. Ed.

in order to encourage the development of the islands by the assurance of safety to investors of capital. All men should be protected in the free exercise of their religion, and the doors thrown open to missionaries of all Christian sects. The land, which belongs to the people, and of which they have been robbed in the past, should be returned to them and their titles made secure. We should inaugurate and carry forward, in the most earnest and liberal way, a comprehensive system of popular education. Finally, while we bring prosperity to the islands by developing their resources, we should, as rapidly as conditions will permit, bestow upon them self-government and home rule. Such, in outline, is the policy which I believe can be and will be pursued toward the Philippines. It will require time, patience, honesty, and ability for its completion, but it is thoroughly practicable and reasonable.

The foundation of it all is the retention of the islands by the United States, and it is to that question that I desire to address myself. The opposition . . . assert that on moral grounds we have no right to take or retain the Philippines, and that as a matter of expediency our whole Eastern policy is a costly mistake. I deny both propositions. I believe we are in the Philippines as righteously as we are there rightfully and legally. I believe that to abandon the islands, or to leave them now, would be a wrong to humanity, a dereliction of duty, a base betrayal of the Filipinos who have supported us, led by the best men of Luzon, and in the highest degree contrary to sound morals. As to expediency, the arguments in favor of the retention of the Philippines seem to me so overwhelming that I should regard their loss as a calamity to our trade and commerce and to all our business interests so great that no man can measure it. Let me take these propositions in their order, beginning with the question of right and wrong, of morals and duty, involved in our action.

Our opponents put forward as their chief objection that we have robbed these people of their liberty and have taken them and hold them in defiance of the doctrine of the Declaration of Independence in regard to the consent of the governed. As to liberty, they have never had it, and have none now, except when we give it to them protected by the flag and the armies of the United States. Their insurrection against Spain, confined to one island, had been utterly abortive and could never have revived or been successful while Spain controlled the sea. We have given them all the liberty they ever had. We could not have robbed them of it, for they had none to lose.

The second objection as to the consent of the governed requires more careful examination. We must go a step farther and see how the American people throughout their history have applied this principle to the vast territory which they have acquired. Under the guidance of Thomas Jefferson, and with a Congress obedient to his slightest behest, we took Louisiana without the consent of the governed, and ruled it without their consent so long as we saw fit.

A few years more passed, and, in 1819, we bought Florida from Spain without the consent of the governed. Then came the Mexican war, and by the treaty of Guadalupe Hidalgo we received a great cession of territory from Mexico, including all the California coast; and although we paid Mexico twenty millions as indemnity I think it has been held that the cession was one of conquest. There were many Mexicans living within the ceded territory. We never asked their consent. In 1867 we purchased Alaska from Russia, territory, people and all. It will be observed that to the white inhabitants we allow the liberty of returning to Russia, but we except the uncivilized tribes specifically. They are to be governed without their consent, and they are not even to be allowed to become citizens.

If the arguments which have been offered against our taking the Philippine Islands because we have not the consent of the inhabitants be just, then our whole past record of expansion is a crime. I do not think that we violated in that record the principles of the Declaration of Independence. On the contrary, I think we spread them over regions where they were unknown. Guided by the principles of that record, I am proud of the treaty of Paris, which is but a continuance of our American policy. The taking of the Philippines does not violate the principles of the Declaration of Independence, but will spread them among a people who have never known liberty and who in a few years will be as unwilling to leave the shelter of the American flag as those of any other territory we ever brought beneath its folds.

The next argument of the opponents of the Republican policy is that we are denying self-government to the Filipinos. Our reply is that to give independent self-government at once, as we understand it, to a people who have no just conception of it and no fitness for it, is to dower them with a curse instead of a blessing. To do this would be to entirely arrest their progress instead of advancing them on the road to the liberty and free government which we wish them to achieve and enjoy. This contention rests, of course, on the proposition that the Filipinos are not today in the least fitted for self-government, as we understand it.

The form of government natural to the Asiatic has always been a despotism. It is perhaps possible for an extremely clever and superior people like the Japanese, with their unsurpassed capacity of imitation, to adopt Western forms of government, but whether the underlying conceptions — which are the only solid foundation of free institutions — can exist under such circumstances is yet to be proved, and all human experience is against the theory. Some of the inhabitants of the Philippines, who have had the benefit of Christianity and of a measure of education, will, I have no doubt, under our fostering care and with peace and order, assume at once a degree of self-government and advance constantly, with our aid, toward a still larger exercise of that inestimable privilege, but to abandon those islands is to leave them to anarchy, to short-lived military dictatorships, to the struggle of factions, and, in a very brief time, to their seizure by some great Western power who will not be at all desirous to train them in the principles of freedom, as we are, but who will take them because the world is no longer large enough to permit some of its most valuable portions to lie barren and ruined, the miserable results of foolish political experiments.

I come now to a consideration of the advantages to the United States involved in our acquisition and retention of the Philippine Islands. Whatever duty to others might seem to demand, I should pause long before supporting any policy if there were the slightest suspicion that it was not for the benefit of the people of the United States. I conceive my first duty to be always to the American people, and I have ever considered it the cardinal principle of American statesmanship to advocate policies which would operate for the benefit of the people of the United States, and most particularly for the advantage of our farmers and our workmen, upon whose well-being, and upon whose full employment at the highest wages, our entire fabric of society and government rests. In a policy which gives us a foothold in the East, which will open a new market in the Philippines, and enable us to increase our commerce with China, I see great advantages to all our people, and more especially to our farmers and our workingmen.

The disadvantages which are put forward seem to me unreal or at best trivial. Dark pictures are drawn of the enormously increased expense of the Navy and of the Army which will be necessitated by these new possessions. So far as the Navy goes, our present fleet is now entirely inadequate for our own needs.

The Philippines will entail upon us no naval expenses that we should not have in any event with a proper naval establishment. But the great bugbear is the Army. Enormous sums have been stated here, all of them mere guesswork, to represent the increased expense to which we have been put by the call for troops for the Philippines. There is no reason to doubt that in a comparatively short time peace and order will be restored, and when we are considering what burden the possession of the islands will impose upon us we must proceed upon the normal conditions of peace. Spain found less than 15,000 men sufficient, and I think it is safe to say that if Spain was able to manage with 15,000 men, the same number of American soldiers would be enough to do very well what Spain did very badly.

As to the expense involved, it seems to be entirely forgotten that the islands themselves are abundantly able to pay for the establishment there, both civil and military. Under Spanish rule, with all its bad administration and profound corruption the islands not only paid all their expenses, but made at times at least a return to the Spanish treasury. With revenues well and honestly administered, and with wise and honest expenditure, the islands in our hands would not only easily pay all the expenses of the military establishment, but of the civil government as well, and we could at the same time, by our superior honesty and efficiency, greatly lighten the burden of taxation. In a word, the Philippine Islands, as we should govern and administer them, would be entirely self-supporting, and would throw no burden of expense at all on the people of the United States after peace and order were once restored and business was again flowing in its normal channels.

So much for the objections commonly made to our Philippine policy, which have as little foundation, in my opinion, as those which proceed on the theory that we are engaged in the perpetration of a great wrong. Let us now look at the other side, and there, I believe, we shall find arguments in favor of the retention of the Philippines as possessions of great value and a source of great profit to the people of the United States which can not be overthrown.

First, as to the islands themselves. They are over a hundred thousand square miles in extent, and are of the greatest richness and fertility. From these islands comes now the best hemp in the world, and there is no tropical product which can not be raised there in abundance. Their forests are untouched, of great extent, and with a variety of hard woods of almost unexampled value. Gold is found throughout all the islands, but not in large quantities, and there is no indication that the production of gold could ever reach a very great amount. There appears to be little or no silver. There are regions in Luzon containing great and valuable deposits of copper which have never been developed. But the chief mineral value of the islands is in their undeveloped coal beds, which are known to exist in certain parts and are believed to exist everywhere, and which are certainly very extensive and rich. The coal is said to be lignite, and, although 20 to 30 per cent inferior to our coals or to those of Cardiff, is practically as good as the Australian coal and better than that of Japan, both of which are largely used in the East today. To a naval and commercial power the coal measures of the Philippines will be a source of great strength and of equally great value. It is sufficient for me to indicate these few elements of natural wealth in the islands which only await development.

A much more important point is to be found in the markets which they furnish. The total value of exports and imports for 1896 amounted in round numbers to $29,000,000, and this was below the average. The exports were nearly $20,000,000, the imports a little over $9,000,000. We took from the Philippines exports to the value of $4,308,000, next in amount to the exports to Great Britain, but the Philippine Islands took from us imports to the value of only $94,000. There can be no doubt that the islands in our peaceful possession would take from us a very large proportion of their imports.

Even as the islands are today there is opportunity for a large absorption of products of the United States, but it must not be forgotten that the islands are entirely undeveloped. The people consume foreign imports at the rate of only a trifle more than $1 per capita. With the development of the islands and the increase of commerce and of business activity the consumption of foreign imports would rapidly advance, and of this increase we should reap the chief benefit. We shall also find great profit in the work of developing the islands. They require railroads everywhere. Those railroads would be planned by American engineers, the rails and the bridges would come from American mills, the locomotives and cars from American workshops. The same would hold true in regard to electric railways, electric lighting, telegraphs, telephones, and steamships for the local business.

An increase of $25,000,000 in our exports to the islands may strike some lofty minds as "sordid." To me that increase means wages and employment to a large number of American farmers and workingmen, and I therefore regard it as of the highest beneficence and importance, and as a striking justification of the policy which finds in our possession of these islands not only advantages to their inhabitants, but an expansion of trade of great profit and value to American labor and American industry.

But the value of the Philippine Islands, both natural and acquired, and as a market for our products, great as it undoubtedly is, and greater as it unquestionably will be, is trifling compared to the indirect results which will flow from our possession of them. From the time of the war between China and Japan it became apparent that great changes were impending in the East, changes which many economists and publicists believed would play the master part in the history of the next century. The struggle for the world's trade, which has for many years been shaping ever more strongly the politics and the history of mankind, has its richest prize set before it in the vast markets of China. Every great nation has recognized the importance of this prize, either by the acquisition of Chinese territory or by obtaining certain rights and privileges through treaty. But after the war between China and Japan this movement rapidly assumed an acute form. It grew daily more apparent that Russia was closing in upon the Chinese Empire, and that her policy, at once slow and persistent, aimed at nothing less than the exclusion of other nations from the greatest market of the world.

To us, with our increasing population, and an agricultural and industrial production which was advancing by leaps and bounds, the need of new markets in the very near future, if we hoped to maintain full employment and ample returns to our farmers and our workingmen, was very clear. More than ready to take our change in a fair field against all rivals, and with full faith in the indomitable ingenuity and enterprise of our people, it was more than ever important that we should not be shut out from any market by unjust or peculiar discriminations if by any methods such a misfortune could be avoided. The great danger to our interests in China became clearer and clearer as the months went by to those who watched the progress of great economic and political forces outside our own boundaries.

I am quite sure that nobody saw very clearly how we were to assert in the East our rights and interests which were so important to the welfare of our agriculture and our industry. That Hawaii was necessary as the first and essential step toward our obtaining that share to which we were entitled in the trade of the Pacific, the ocean of the future, was obvious enough, but beyond that all was doubt and darkness. Then came the Spanish war, and the smoke of Dewey's guns had hardly cleared away when it was seen by those who were watching that he had not only destroyed the Spanish fleet, but had given to his countrymen the means of solving their problem in the Far East. He had made us an Eastern power. He had given us not only the right to speak, but the place to speak from.

Let me now try to show the importance and meaning of the Eastern question, with regard to which Dewey's victory has given us such a commanding position. The Empire of China has a population of which we have no accurate statistics, but which is certainly over four hundred millions. The rate of consumption among the Chinese per capita is at present low, but even as it stands it affords a great market for foreign imports. The work of opening up the country by railroads and of developing its still untouched natural resources has begun and is advancing with giant strides. There is the greatest opportunity in China for trade expansion which exists anywhere in the world. I desire to call the attention of the Senate to the value of the Chinese trade to us now despite our neglect of it, and to the enormous advance which that trade has made in the last four years, and more especially since the Spanish war carried our flag into the East and turned the attention of our people more sharply to the unlimited opportunities for commerce which there exist.

It will be seen that our exports to China and Hongkong in 1899 were over $22,000,000, and that the growth in the last three years had been phenomenal. The gain in exports to China, Hongkong, and Japan in 1899 over 1889 was 256 per cent, and it almost all came in the last years of the decade.

There are two points, however, to which I wish to call especial attention, because they emphasize and demonstrate the great value to our farming and manufacturing interests of this vast Chinese market into which we are just entering. In 1898 we sent nearly four million dollars' worth of wheat flour to Hongkong alone. while to China we sent $5,203,427 worth of cotton manufactures in the same year and [totaling] over $9,000,000 worth, as compared with only $2,854,221 worth for 1894.

These are illustrations in two leading articles of what the Chinese market means to the Western growers of wheat and to the manufacturers of cotton. From these two items as well as from the long lists of Mr. Hitchcock we can judge what the trade of China is to us to-day and what it is destined to be. The loss of that market and of its prospects and possibilities I should regard as one of the greatest calamities which could befall the farmers and the workingmen of the United States. How, then, are we to hold and develop it? Look at your tables of statistics and note the increases which have occurred since the capture of Manila. The mere fact that we hold the Philippine Islands increases our trade with all the East — with China and Japan alike.

But we must go a step further. Having this opportunity to obtain a large and increasing share in the trade of China, how shall we make sure that it is not taken from us? We know well that China is threatened by Russia, and that Russian dominion, if unrestrained, would mean discrimination and exclusion in the Chinese markets. Sooner than anyone dreamed it has been shown how far the Philippines have solved this pressing problem for us. The possession of the Philippines made us an Eastern power, with the right and, what was equally important, the force behind the right to speak.

Mr. Hay, as Secretary of State, has obtained from all the great powers of Europe their assent to our demand for the guaranty of all our treaty rights in China and for the maintenance of the policy of the open door. I do not belittle one of the most important and most brilliant diplomatic achievements in our hundred years of national existence when I say that the assent of these other powers to the propositions of the United States was given to the master of Manila. They might have turned us aside three years ago with a shrug and a smile, but to the power which held Manila Bay, and whose fleet floated upon its waters, they were obliged to give a gracious answer. Manila, with its magnificent bay, is the prize and the pearl of the East. In our hands it will become one of the greatest distributing points, one of the richest emporiums of the world's commerce. Rich in itself, with all its fertile islands behind it, it will keep open to us the markets of China and enable American enterprise and intelligence to take a master share in all the trade of the Orient.

We have been told that arguments like these are sordid. Sordid indeed! Then what arguments are worthy of consideration? A policy which proposes to open wider markets to the people of the United States, to add to their employment, and to increase their wages, and which in its pursuit requires that we should save the teeming millions of China from the darkness of the Russian winter, and keep them free, not merely for the incoming of commerce, but for the entrance of the light of Western civilization, seems to me a great and noble policy, if there ever was such, and one which may well engage the best aspirations and the highest abilities of American statesmanship.

Thus, Mr. President, I have shown that duty and interest alike, duty of the highest kind and interest of the highest and best kind, impose upon us the retention of the Philippines, the development of the islands, and the expansion of our Eastern commerce. All these things, in my belief, will come to pass, whatever the divisions of the present moment, for no people who have come under our flag have ever sought to leave it, and there is no territory which we have acquired that any one would dream of giving up.

All our vast growth and expansion have been due to the spirit of our race, and have been guided by the instinct of the American people, which in all great crises has proved wiser than any reasoning. This mighty movement westward, building up a nation and conquering a continent as it swept along, has not been the work of chance or accident. It was neither chance nor accident which brought us to the Pacific and which has now carried us across the great ocean even to the shores of Asia, to the very edge of the cradle of the Aryans, whence our far distant ancestors started on the march which has since girdled the world.

Like every great nation, we have come more than once in our history to where the road of fate divided. Thus far we have never failed to take the right path. Again are we come to the parting of the ways. Again a momentous choice is offered to us. Shall we hesitate and make, in coward fashion, what Dante calls "the great refusal"?

Even now we can abandon the Monroe Doctrine, we can reject the Pacific, we can shut ourselves up between our oceans, as Switzerland is inclosed among her hills, and then it would be inevitable that we should sink out from among the great powers of the world and heap up riches that some stronger and bolder people, who do not fear their fate, might gather them. Or we may follow the true laws of our being, the laws in obedience to which we have come to be what we are, and then we shall stretch out into the Pacific; we shall stand in the front rank of the world powers; we shall give to our labor and our industry new and larger and better opportunities; we shall prosper ourselves; we shall benefit mankind. What we have done was inevitable because it was in accordance with the laws of our being as a nation, in the defiance and disregard of which lie ruin and retreat.

Carl Schurz: AMERICAN IMPERIALISM

AN ADDRESS OPPOSING ANNEXATION OF THE PHILIPPINES, JANUARY 4, 1899

IT is proposed to embark this republic in a course of imperialistic policy by permanently annexing to it certain islands taken, or partly taken, from Spain in the late war. The matter is near its decision, but not yet decided. The peace treaty made at Paris is not yet ratified by the Senate; but even if it were, the question whether those islands, although ceded by Spain, shall be permanently incorporated in the territory of the United States would still be open for final determination by Congress. As an open question therefore I shall discuss it.

If ever, it behooves the American people to think and act with calm delib-

From Carl Schurz, *American Imperialism* (The Convocation Address delivered on the occasion of the Twenty-seventh Convocation of the University of Chicago, January 4, 1899), pp. 3–4, 5–6, 7, 9–10, 11, 15, 17–18, 20–21, 25–34.

eration, for the character and future of the republic and the welfare of its people now living and yet to be born are in unprecedented jeopardy. To form a candid judgment of what this republic has been, what it may become, and what it ought to be, let us first recall to our minds its condition before the recent Spanish War.

Our government was, in the words of Abraham Lincoln, "the government of the people, by the people, and for the people." It was the noblest ambition of all true Americans to carry this democratic government to the highest degree of perfection and justice, in probity, in assured peace, in the security of human rights, in progressive civilization; to solve the problem of popular self-government on the grandest scale, and thus to make this republic the example and guiding star of mankind. . . .

Such was our condition, such our beliefs and ideals, such our ambition and our pride, but a short year ago. . . .

Then came the Spanish War. A few vigorous blows laid the feeble enemy helpless at our feet. The whole scene seemed to have suddenly changed. According to the solemn proclamation of our government, the war had been undertaken solely for the liberation of Cuba, as a war of humanity and not of conquest. But our easy victories had put conquest within our reach, and when our arms occupied foreign territory, a loud demand arose that, pledge or no pledge to the contrary, the conquests should be kept, even the Philippines on the other side of the globe, and that as to Cuba herself, independence would only be a provisional formality. Why not? was the cry. Has not the career of the republic almost from its very beginning been one of territorial expansion? Has it not acquired Louisiana, Florida, Texas, the vast countries that came to us through the Mexican

War, and Alaska, and has it not digested them well? Were not those acquisitions much larger than those now in contemplation? If the republic could digest the old, why not the new? What is the difference?

Only look with an unclouded eye, and you will soon discover differences enough warning you to beware. There are five of decisive importance.

1. All the former acquisitions were on this continent, and, excepting Alaska, contiguous to our borders.

2. They were situated, not in the tropical, but in the temperate zone, where democratic institutions thrive, and where our people could migrate in mass.

3. They were but very thinly peopled — in fact, without any population that would have been in the way of new settlement.

4. They could be organized as territories in the usual manner, with the expectation that they would presently come into the Union as self-governing states with populations substantially homogeneous to our own.

5. They did not require a material increase of our army or navy, either for their subjection to our rule or for their defense against any probable foreign attack provoked by their being in our possession. . . .

Compare now with our old acquisitions as to all these important points those at present in view.

They are not continental, not contiguous to our present domain, but beyond seas, the Philippines many thousand miles distant from our coast. They are all situated in the tropics, where people of the northern races, such as Anglo-Saxons, or, generally speaking, people of Germanic blood, have never migrated in mass to stay; and they are more or less densely populated, parts of them as densely as

Massachusetts — their populations consisting almost exclusively of races to whom the tropical climate is congenial — Spanish creoles mixed with negroes in the West Indies, and Malays, Tagals, Filipinos, Chinese, Japanese, Negritos, and various more or less barbarous tribes in the Philippines. . . .

What, then, shall we do with such populations? Shall we, according, not indeed to the letter, but to the evident spirit of our constitution, organize those countries as territories with a view to their eventual admission as states? If they become states on an equal footing with the other states they will not only be permitted to govern themselves as to their home concerns, but they will take part in governing the whole republic, in governing us, by sending senators and representatives into our Congress to help make our laws, and by voting for president and vice-president to give our national government its executive. The prospect of the consequences which would follow the admission of the Spanish creoles and the negroes of West India islands and of the Malays and Tagals of the Philippines to participation in the conduct of our government is so alarming that you instinctively pause before taking the step.

But this may be avoided, it is said, by governing the new possessions as mere dependencies, or subject provinces. I will waive the constitutional question and merely point out that this would be a most serious departure from the rule that governed our former acquisitions, which are so frequently quoted as precedents. It is useless to speak of the District of Columbia and Alaska as proof that we have done such things before and can do them again. Every candid mind will at once admit the vast difference between those cases and the *permanent* establishment of substantially arbitrary government over large territories with many millions of inhabitants, and with a prospect of there being many more of the same kind, if we once launch out on a career of conquest. The question is not merely whether we *can* do such things, but whether, having the public good at heart, we *should* do them.

If we do adopt such a system, then we shall, for the first time since the abolition of slavery, again have two kinds of Americans: Americans of the first class, who enjoy the privilege of taking part in the government in accordance with our old constitutional principles, and Americans of the second class, who are to be ruled in a substantially arbitrary fashion by the Americans of the first class, through congressional legislation and the action of the national executive — not to speak of individual "masters" arrogating to themselves powers beyond the law. . . .

If we do, we shall transform the government of the people, for the people, and by the people, for which Abraham Lincoln lived, into a government of one part of the people, the strong, over another part, the weak. Such an abandonment of a fundamental principle as a permanent policy may at first seem to bear only upon more or less distant dependencies, but it can hardly fail in its ultimate effects to disturb the rule of the same principle in the conduct of democratic government at home. And I warn the American people that a democracy cannot so deny its faith as to the vital conditions of its being — it cannot long play the king over subject populations without creating within itself ways of thinking and habits of action most dangerous to its own vitality — most dangerous especially to those classes of society which are the least powerful in the assertion, and the most helpless in the defense of their rights. Let the poor and the men who earn their bread by the labor of their hands pause and consider well before they give their assent to a policy so deliberately forgetful of the equality of rights. . . .

Our old acquisitions did not require a material increase of our army and navy. What of the new? It is generally admitted that we need very considerable additions to our armaments on land and sea to restore and keep order on the islands taken from Spain, and then to establish our sovereignty there. This is a ticklish business. In the first place, Spain has never been in actual control and possession of a good many of the Philippine islands, while on others the insurgent Filipinos had well-nigh destroyed the Spanish power when the treaty of Paris was made. The people of those islands will either peaceably submit to our role or they will not. If they do not, and we must conquer them by force of arms, we shall at once have war on our hands. . . .

If we take those new regions, we shall be well entangled in that contest for territorial aggrandizement, which distracts other nations and drives them far beyond their original design. So it will be inevitably with us. We shall want new conquests to protect that which we already possess. The greed of speculators working upon our government, will push us from one point to another, and we shall have new conflicts on our hands, almost without knowing how we got into them. It has always been so under such circumstances, and always will be. This means more and more soldiers, ships, and guns.

A singular delusion has taken hold of the minds of otherwise clear-headed men. It is that our new friendship with England will serve firmly to secure the world's peace. Nobody can hail that friendly feeling between the two nations more warmly than I do, and I fervidly hope it will last. But I am profoundly convinced that if this friendship results in the two

countries setting out to grasp "for the Anglo-Saxon," as the phrase is, whatever of the earth may be attainable — if they hunt in couple — they will surely soon fall out about the game, and the first serious quarrel, or at least one of the first, we shall have, will be with Great Britain. And as family feuds are the bitterest, that feud will be apt to become one of the most deplorable in its consequences.

No nation is, or ought to be, unselfish. England, in her friendly feeling toward us, is not inspired by mere sentimental benevolence. The anxious wish of many Englishmen that we should take the Philippines is not free from the consideration that, if we do so, we shall for a long time depend on British friendship to maintain our position on that field of rivalry, and that Britain will derive ample profit from our dependence on her. . . .

Let this republic and Great Britain each follow the course which its conditions and its history have assigned to it, and their ambitions will not clash, and their friendships can be maintained for the good of all. And if our British cousins should ever get into serious stress, American friendship may stand behind them; but then Britain would depend on our friendship, which, as an American, I should prefer, and not America on British friendship, as our British friends who so impatiently urge us to take the Philippines, would have it. But if we do take the Philippines, and thus entangle ourselves in the rivalries of Asiatic affairs, the future will be, as Lord Salisbury predicted, one of wars and rumors of wars, and the time will be forever past when we could look down with condescending pity on the nations of the old world groaning under militarism with all its burdens. . . .

What can there be to justify a change of policy fraught with such direful consequences? Let us pass the arguments of the advocates of such imperialism candidly in review.

The cry suddenly raised that this great country has become too small for us is too ridiculous to demand an answer, in view of the fact that our present population may be tripled and still have ample elbow-room, with resources to support many more. But we are told that our industries are gasping for breath; that we are suffering from over-production; that our products must have new outlets, and that we need colonies and dependencies the world over to give us more markets. More markets? Certainly. But do we, civilized beings, indulge in the absurd and barbarous notion that we must own the countries with which we wish to trade? Here are our official reports before us, telling us that of late years our export trade has grown enormously, not only of farm products, but of the products of our manufacturing industries; in fact, that "our sales of manufacturing goods have continued to extend with a facility and promptitude of results which have excited the serious concern of countries that, for generations, had not only controlled their home markets, but had practically monopolized certain lines of trade in other lands.". . .

"But the Pacific Ocean," we are mysteriously told, "will be the great commercial battlefield of the future, and we must quickly use the present opportunity to secure our position on it. The visible presence of great power is necessary for us to get our share of the trade of China. Therefore, we must have the Philippines." Well, the China trade is worth having, although for a time out of sight the Atlantic Ocean will be an infinitely more important battlefield of commerce than the Pacific, and one European customer is worth more than twenty or thirty Asiatics. But does the trade of China really require that we should have the Philippines and make a great display of power to get our share? Read the consular reports, and you will find that in many places in China our trade is rapidly gaining, while in some British trade is declining, and this while Great Britain had on hand the greatest display of power imaginable and we had none. And in order to increase our trade there, our consuls advise us to improve our commercial methods, saying nothing of the necessity of establishing a base of naval operations, and of our appearing there with war ships and heavy guns. Trade is developed, not by the best guns, but by the best merchants. But why do other nations prepare to fight for the Chinese trade? Other nations have done many foolish things which we have been, and I hope will remain, wise enough not to imitate. If it should come to fighting for Chinese customers, the powers engaged in that fight are not unlikely to find out that they pay too high a price for what can be gained, and that at last the peaceful and active NEUTRAL will have the best bargain. At any rate, to launch into all the embroilments of an imperialistic policy by annexing the Philippines in order to snatch something more of the Chinese trade would be for us the foolishest game of all.

Generally speaking, nothing could be more irrational than all the talk about our losing commercial or other opportunities which "will never come back if we fail to grasp them now." Why, we are so rapidly growing in all the elements of power ahead of all other nations that, not many decades hence, unless we demoralize ourselves by a reckless policy of adventure, not one of them will be able to resist our will if we choose to enforce it. This the world knows, and is alarmed at the prospect. Those who are most alarmed may wish that we should give them now, by some rash enterprise, an occasion for dealing us a damaging blow while we are less irresistible.

"But we must have coaling stations for our navy!" Well, can we not get as many coaling stations as we need without owning populous countries behind them that would entangle us in dangerous political responsibilities and complications? Must Great Britain own the whole of Spain in order to hold Gibraltar?

"But we must civilize those poor people!" Are we not ingenious and charitable enough to do much for their civilization without subjugating and ruling them by criminal aggression?

The rest of the pleas for imperialism consist mostly of those high-sounding catch-words of which a free people when about to decide a great question should be especially suspicious. We are admonished that it is time for us to become a "world power." Well, we *are* a world power now, and have been for many years. What is a world power? A power strong enough to make its voice listened to with deference by the world whenever it chooses to speak. Is it necessary for a world power, in order to be such, to have its finger in every pie? Must we have the Philippines in order to become a world power? To ask the question is to answer it. . . .

But, they tell us, we have been living in a state of contemptible isolation which must be broken so that we may feel and conduct ourselves "as a full-grown member of the family of nations." What is that so-called isolation? Is it commercial? Last year our foreign trade amounted to nearly 2000 million dollars, and is rapidly growing. Is that commercial isolation? Or are we politically isolated? Remember our history. Who was it that early in this century broke up the piracy of the Barbary

States? Who was it that took a leading part in delivering the world's commerce of the Danish Sound dues? Who was it that first opened Japan to communication with the western world? And what power has in this century made more valuable contributions to international law than the United States? Do you call that contemptible isolation? It is true, we did not meddle much with foreign affairs that did not concern us. But if the circle of our interests widens and we wish to meddle more, must we needs have the Philippines in order to feel and conduct ourselves as a member of the family of nations? . . .

You may tell me that this is all very well, but that by the acts of our own government we are now in this annexation business, and how can we get decently out of it? I answer that the difficulties of getting out of it may be great; but that they are infinitely less great than the difficulties we shall have to contend with if we stay in it.

Looking them in the face, let us first clear our minds of confused notions about our duties and responsibilities in the premises. That our victories have devolved upon us certain duties as to the people of the conquered islands, I readily admit. But are they the only duties we have to perform, or have they suddenly become paramount to all other duties? I deny it. I deny that the duties we owe to the Cubans and the Porto Ricans and the Filipinos and the Tagals of the Asiatic islands absolve us from our duties to the 75 millions of our own people and to their posterity. I deny that they oblige us to destroy the moral credit of our own republic by turning this loudly heralded war of liberation and humanity into a land-grabbing game and an act of criminal aggression. I deny that they compel us to aggravate our race troubles, to bring upon us the constant danger of war, and to subject our people to the galling burden of increasing armaments. . . .

They fought for deliverance from Spanish oppression, and we helped them to obtain that deliverance. That deliverance they understood to mean independence. I repeat the question whether anybody can tell me why the declaration of Congress that the Cubans *of right ought to be* free and independent should not apply to all of them? Their independence, therefore, would be the natural and rightful outcome. This is the solution of the problem first to be taken in view.

It is objected that they are not capable of independent government. They may answer that this is their affair and that they are at least entitled to a trial. I frankly admit that if they are given that trial, their conduct in governing themselves will be far from perfect. Well, the conduct of no people is perfect, not even our own. They may try to revenge themselves upon their tories in their Revolutionary War. But we, too, threw our tories into hideous dungeons during our Revolutionary War and persecuted and drove them away after its close. They may have bloody civil broils. But we, too, have had our Civil War which cost hundreds and thousands of lives and devastated one-half of our land; and now we have in horrible abundance the killings by lynch law, and our battles at Virden. They may have troubles with their wild tribes. So had we, and we treated our wild tribes in a manner not to be proud of. They may have corruption and rapacity in their government, but Havana and Ponce may get municipal administration almost as good as New York has under Tammany rule; and Manila may secure a city council not much less virtuous than that of Chicago.

I say these things not in a spirit of levity, well understanding the difference; but I say them seriously to remind you that, when we speak of the government those islands should have, we cannot reasonably set up standards which are not reached even by the most civilized people, and which in those regions could not be reached, even if we ourselves conducted their government with our best available statesmanship. Our attention is in these days frequently called to the admirable and in many respects successful administrative machinery introduced by Great Britain in India. But it must not be forgotten that this machinery was evolved from a century of rapine, corruption, disastrous blunders, savage struggles, and murderous revolts, and that even now many wise men in England gravely doubt in their hearts whether it was best for their country to undertake the conquest of India at all, and are troubled by gloomy forebodings of a calamitous catastrophe that may some day engulf that splendid fabric of Asiatic dominion.

No, we cannot expect that the Porto Ricans, the Cubans, and the Filipinos will maintain orderly governments in Anglo-Saxon fashion. But they may succeed in establishing a tolerable order of things in their own fashion, as Mexico, after many decades of turbulent disorder, succeeded at last, under Porfirio Diaz, in having a strong and orderly government of her kind, not, indeed, such a government as we would tolerate in this Union, but a government answering Mexican character and interests, and respectable in its relations with the outside world.

This will become all the more possible if, without annexing and ruling those people, we simply put them on their feet, and then give them the benefit of that humanitarian spirit which, as we claim, led us into the war for the liberation of Cuba. To this end we should keep our troops on the islands only until their people have constructed governments and organized forces of their own for the maintenance of order. Our military occupation should not be kept up as long as possible, but should be withdrawn as soon as possible.

The Philippines may, as Belgium and Switzerland are in Europe, be covered by a guarantee of neutrality on the part of the powers most interested in that region — an agreement which the diplomacy of the United States should not find it difficult to obtain. This would secure them against foreign aggression. As to the independent republics of Porto Rico and Cuba, our government might lend its good offices to unite them with San Domingo and Haiti in a confederacy of the Antilles, to give them a more respectable international standing. Stipulations should be agreed upon with them as to open ports and the freedom of business enterprise within their borders, affording all possible commercial facilities. Missionary effort in the largest sense, as to the development of popular education and of other civilizing agencies, as well as abundant charity in case of need, will on our part not be wanting, and all this will help to mitigate their disorderly tendencies and to steady their governments.

Thus we shall be their best friends without being their foreign rulers. We shall have done our duty to them, to ourselves, and to the world. However imperfect their governments may still remain, they will at least be their own, and they will not with their disorders and corruptions contaminate our institutions, the integrity of which is not only to ourselves, but to liberty-loving mankind, the most important concern of all. We may then await the result with generous patience — with the same patience with which for many years we witnessed the revolutionary disorders of Mexico on our very borders, without any thought of taking her government into our own hands.

Ask yourselves whether a policy like this will not raise the American people to a level of moral greatness never before attained! If this democracy, after all the intoxication of triumph in war, conscientiously remembers its professions and pledges, and soberly reflects on its duties to itself and others, and then deliberately resists the temptation of conquest, it will achieve the grandest triumph of the democratic idea that history knows of....

Samuel F. Bemis:

THE GREAT ABERRATION OF 1898

WITH the three months' warfare which began in April, 1898, collapsed the final remnants of Spanish power in the Indies, West and East, almost the last bits of that great empire sanctioned by the treaty of Tordesillas of 1494, with which we began this history. For this decisive conflict the military preparedness of the United States was woefully disproportionate to the martial

From Samuel F. Bemis, *A Diplomatic History of the United States*, 3rd ed., pp. 463–475. By permission of Henry Holt and Company, copyright 1936, 1942, and 1950. NOTE: For footnotes see the original. Ed.

spirit, but the new navy proved to be in fighting trim, and it was sea power which decided the issue. There was a small Spanish squadron in the Philippines; this was almost immediately destroyed in the battle of Manila Bay (May 1, 1898) by a superior American force which had been carefully prepared and stationed in Far Eastern waters under the command of Commodore George Dewey. From the remaining naval forces of Spain in Europe a fleet under Admiral Cervera steamed to the Caribbean and took refuge, by bad strategy, in the bottleneck harbor of Santiago de Cuba, where it was immediately blockaded by the American fleet under Admiral Sampson. A valorous but ill-trained expeditionary force of 16,000 troops commanded by Major-General Shafter, including a volunteer regiment of "Rough Riders" under Colonel Leonard Wood and Lieutenant-Colonel Theodore Roosevelt, who had just resigned as Assistant Secretary of the Navy, and not excluding a large company of enthusiastic war correspondents, landed in the environs of Santiago and besieged the city. Cervera's ships filed out of the bottleneck in an heroic effort to battle their way through the American fleet, only to meet swift and complete destruction (July 3, 1898). Santiago then was surrendered. Meanwhile a small expeditionary force had been sufficient to take possession of the Spanish island of Puerto Rico. The fighting was over. War had quickly ended the horrors and destitution of chronic insurrectionary hostilities and saved thereby the lives of hundreds of thousands, not only of Spanish soldiers, but of Cuban *insurrectos* and civilian population, men, women, and children. It was in this sense a merciful war.

The decisive military events convinced the Spanish Government and people that to fight further was hopeless. Through the intermediary of the French Republic, and its ambassador in Washington, Spain asked for an armistice, which was signed August 12, under terms dictated by the victor. Spain relinquished all claim of sovereignty over the island of Cuba, and agreed to cede to the United States, Puerto Rico and one island of the Ladrone group in the west Pacific to be selected by the United States, and immediately to evacuate Cuba and Puerto Rico and all Spanish islands in the West Indies. The status of the Philippines was left to the peace conference which was called to meet in Paris not later than October 1. The armistice stated that meanwhile the United States would "occupy and hold the city, bay and harbor of Manila pending the conclusion of a treaty of peace which shall determine the control, disposition, and government of the Philippines."

Before we consider the fateful decision which the United States had to make, it is best to notice the circumstances of Dewey's presence in the islands before and after his victory, and his relations with the native insurrectionary leaders and with foreign powers, notably Germany. Dewey's station in command of an American squadron in the Far East, in readiness for offensive operations in case of war with Spain, was due to the foresight of the young and alert Assistant Secretary of the Navy, Theodore Roosevelt. He had successfully pulled wires to get Dewey appointed to command of the Pacific squadron and had seen that his ships were well prepared for the contemplated action. Before sailing from Hong Kong for the historic naval action at Manila Bay, Commodore Dewey got in touch with certain Filipino insurrectionists, led by Emilio Aguinaldo, who had been exiled from the islands. The Commodore saw that they might be useful in undermining Spanish authority in the islands. After the destruction of the Spanish squadron, he called Aguinaldo and some of his comrades to Manila and planted them in the island of Luzon. They immediately organized an insurrection, assisted by American arms and ammunition. At no time did any American official make any specific agreement with them that the independence of the Philippines would be established in case Spain should be defeated, but there seems little question that Aguinaldo honestly so understood, and enthusiastically he rallied the natives to the American cause. His troops invested Manila from the land while the American fleet blockaded it from the sea.

During the summer various neutral warships appeared as observers at Manila: on June 17 a German fleet of five vessels under Vice Admiral von Diederichs, at least equal in weight and guns to Dewey's force; a few days later came three British ships under Captain Chichester; there was also a French and a Japanese warship there.

We know from the German diplomatic correspondence published since the World War that the German squadron had been sent to Manila Bay to lend its watchful presence to the hope that Germany might somehow, some day, be able to take over part or all of the Philippines in case the United States did not keep them. "His Majesty, the Emperor," wrote Foreign Minister von Bülow to the Ambassador at Washington, July 1, 1898, "deems it a principal object of German policy to leave unused no opportunity which may arise from the Spanish-American War to obtain naval *fulcra* in East Asia." Germany endeavored to bring about the neutralization of the islands pending a time when events might be propitious for procuring a partition; but she

could not get the co-operation of Great Britain for such a step. At Manila, the German Admiral annoyed Dewey excessively by violating the blockade in various ways, by making a gesture against Aguinaldo's forces, and by opening up communication with the Spanish authorities — he was listening to proposals by the Governor that some neutral power take over the islands in deposit for the duration of the war. The culminating incident of this officious and intrusive conduct occurred on August 13, when, after arrival of an expeditionary force from San Francisco, Dewey took position to shell the Spanish shore batteries, in support of an attack on the defenses of Manila by General Merritt's troops. One of the legends of American history is that on the day of the bombardment Captain Chichester of the British fleet conspicuously moved his vessels in between the Germans and Dewey, as if to serve notice that if Diederich opened fire on Dewey the British men-of-war would come to the American Commodore's defense. After the surrender of Manila (August 13, 1898) the German squadron departed suddenly, to be seen there no more. Germany abandoned hopes of getting anything out of the Philippines in the near future in defiance of the United States and perhaps of England. The appearance of the German squadron in Manila Bay and its unfriendly attitude there lent marked emphasis to the rivalry in imperialism between two new world powers, which was sharpened in the Venezuela affair of 1902, and by the eagerness of the German Admiralty to secure naval bases or maritime *fulcra* in the Caribbean region. German and American naval officers began to measure themselves and their navies against each other. Back of the new rivalry in imperialism lay a mutual popular resentment in each country against the other's high protective tariff system.

The archives are not yet unlocked which will reveal fully the secrets of British foreign policy in 1898 and the inner history of British action at Manila Bay, including Captain Chichester's instructions, if he had any, but this much seems clear: since the Kruger telegram of 1896 Great Britain had changed her outlook and was seeking possible allies to end her increasingly dangerous isolation. It was also to her interest to encourage the United States to take a place physically in the Far Eastern arena where it might support British policy to keep China open to the trade of the Occident, which was predominantly a British commerce.

Anglo-American relations now became more harmonious than at any time since the Revolution. We have already observed how this resulted in the arbitration of outstanding issues, and in later chapters we shall see how it led to the temporary equipoise of the question of China, to the readjustment of the Isthmian Question in line with American desires, and to the cordial reciprocation of the United States toward Great Britain during the Boer War. The foundations for this revived Anglo-American amity were laid in 1896–1898. On her part, Germany, for her own obvious interests, worked without success to break down this new Anglo-American cordiality.

After the signature of the Spanish-American armistice, Germany entered into a secret agreement with Spain (September 10, 1898), dependent upon the results of the war with the United States, for the purchase of the islands of Kusaie, Ponape, and Yap, in the Caroline group. This was followed up (treaties of December 10, 1898, and February 12, 1899) by the actual purchase for $5,000,000 (ptas. 25,000,000) without objection by the United States, of the Carolines, the Pelews, and the Ladrones, except for Guam Island which had been occupied during the war and ceded by the treaty of peace to the United States. They were the last of the Spanish islands left in the Pacific. Germany held them until the World War, when they were conquered by the Japanese. They went to Japanese mandate during Japan's membership in the League of Nations, and remained there in nominal mandate, unchallenged, after Japan's resignation from the League. Of small importance otherwise, they have the greatest strategical value as roosting-places for airplanes and naval bases for submarines, located across the communications from North America to the Philippines. Japan had shown an active interest in the Philippines in 1898. In a note of September 8 to the United States, the Japanese Government, while fully recognizing that the decision of the future of the islands rested with the United States, suggested that if it should feel disinclined to undertake alone the administration of the Philippines, Japan "would be willing to join with the United States, either singly or in conjunction with another Power having identical interests, in the endeavor to form, subject to proper conditions, a suitable government for the territory in question under the joint or tripartite protection of the guaranteeing powers." This offer was politely declined, and not made public. Great Britain too was interested in buying the islands if the United States did not heed British urgings to keep them. It was obvious if the United States stepped out some other power than Spain would step in; perhaps more than one power would jostle each other to get in first. However insufficient, this was one of the reasons which impelled the Administration to continue in control.

After his victory at Manila Bay, Dewey

could have sailed right along home, and it is a pity that he did not. Instead of that he continued to hold Manila Bay and to blockade the city. He suggested that if five thousand troops could be sent he could occupy Manila. Eleven thousand were sent and the city occupied August 13, with only a prearranged sham resistance by the Spanish garrison, which then concerted with the Americans to keep out the Filipino forces, who had helped to beleaguer Manila, and who already controlled most of the remaining parts of the islands. General Merritt had instructions to insure order in the Philippines as long as the United States should hold them, and to avoid any joint occupation with the native insurrectionists. Aguinaldo, feeling that he had been betrayed, organized the formidable two years' insurrection against the American occupants. By the irony of fate, the United States, which fought a war with Spain to end an insurrection in Cuba nearby, soon found itself with an insurrection on its own hands in distant islands on the other side of the globe. The suppression of the insurrection was not without shameful and unnecessary cases of brutality and atrocity which reflect no honor on the individuals concerned, much as they have been condemned by enlightened American public opinion.

In the peace negotiations at Paris there were two essential questions remaining to be settled: the Cuban debt, and the final disposition of the Philippines. Spain had given up Cuba and Puerto Rico already in the armistice of August 12, and was now willing to cede the island of Guam to the United States. She resisted unsuccessfully the American demand that she should assume the debt of Cuba existing in the shape of about $400,000,000 of Spanish bonds, a debt accumulated largely for the political purpose of sub-jecting the island. The great question therefore remaining before President McKinley and his advisers was whether to keep any or all of the Philippines. They were confronted squarely with the issue of outright and undisguised imperialism. This was the most important question in foreign policy which the nation had been called upon to decide since its independence. An absolutely new question, it had to be decided promptly in the fever-time of exuberant war feeling. President Washington a century before had warned his countrymen not to involve themselves in European political questions. The Monroe Doctrine had laid down such abstention as a fundamental principle of American foreign policy. Should the United States now involve itself at once in both European and Asiatic political questions, as it must needs do if it took over the Philippines, assuming vast liabilities in a part of the world where its interests were not vital, treading a political labyrinth where its step was least secure and its vision least luminous? Should it choose the perilous path of imperialism in the Far East, amid lands and peoples so distant from the American system and so alien to it?

Before the war there had not been the slightest demand for the acquisition of the Philippine Islands. The average American citizen could not have told you whether Filipinos were Far Eastern aborigines or a species of tropical nuts. The American people had no more interest in the islands than they have today in Madagascar. At the time of Dewey's victory, President McKinley himself had to look them up on the globe; he could not have told their locality, he said, within two thousand miles. But the expansionists of 1898, the new imperialists, the Roosevelts, the Lodges, the Mahans, the exponents of a "large" policy, knew where the Philippines were and they soon wanted them for the United States, wanted them as a valorous young swain yearns for the immediate object of his feelings, knowing only the passion of the present and seeing only the more appealing allurements of the hour. They inspired the vociferous desires of lesser leaders, and finally the President himself was seduced. Not long after the battle of Manila Bay, Colonel Roosevelt was writing his friend Lodge repeatedly opposing any peace "until we get Puerto Rico, while Cuba is made independent and the Philippines at any rate taken from the Spaniards." Captain Mahan was seeing the problem of Asia as one which must be solved by the tutelage of the Teuton nations, including among them the United States with its own base in the Philippines. In his annual message of 1897 President McKinley had stated, anent Cuba, that forcible annexation was unthinkable, — "that, by our code of morality, would be criminal aggression." This did not prevent him from thinking of annexation of other islands once the war began. "While we are conducting war and until its conclusion," he noted, "we must keep all we get; when the war is over we must keep what we want." What did the country want?

With the victories of American arms, imperialist sentiment had flared up and spread like wildfire, fanned by the psychology and self-esteem that accompanied a victorious war. The press, at first only speculative, became soon fascinated by the precipitate intrusion of American arms into the Far East and began to conjure the possibilities of American dominion over the Philippines. By the end of the summer a strong tone had set in for retaining them. Business leaders, who had opposed the war with Spain, now began to see vistas of trade expansion from it.

Rapidly moving events on the continent of Asia contributed to the quick development of this sentiment. After the Sino-Japanese War of 1895, the powers of Europe intervened, first to stay Japan's foothold on the Liaotung Peninsula, and next (1897–1898) to acquire for themselves fortified naval bases and spheres of territorial interest over China. Germany forced a lease of Tsingtao and fixed her sphere in Shantung. This precipitated action by Russia to secure a lease of Port Arthur and the Liaotung Peninsula and to fasten her influence on Manchuria. Great Britain leased Weihaiwei on the north coast of Shantung, extended her holdings at Kowloon, opposite the British island of Hong Kong, and established her sphere in the Yangtze valley. France obtained a lease of Kwang-chou Bay, and set up a sphere over the island of Hainan and the three southern Chinese provinces (Yunnan, and Kwangsi, and Kwangtung) bordering on French Cochin-China; and Japan, after having been ousted from southern Manchuria by Russia, Germany, and France, extended her sphere over the province of Fukien, opposite the recently conquered island of Formosa. In each instance China was obliged to agree not to sell, lease, hypothecate, or otherwise alienate to any third power any port or territory within the designated sphere.

The normal expectation was that these spheres would soon become protectorates maintained from the naval bases, that their extension and transformation into actual dominion would be only a question of time. In that case all equality of trade would disappear in favor of the partitioning powers in each instance, and (so it was feared) the United States, whose merchants and navigators had long enjoyed most-favored-nation commercial privileges by treaties with China made in the wake of western wars against that

Empire, would finally be left out in the cold. Let it be said, too, that each of the European powers, notably Great Britain, was more or less impelled to establish its sphere for fear that a rival would dominate China exclusively.

With China thus on the brink of partition the Spanish-American War fortuitously and coincidently placed the American navy in control of Manila Bay and with it the whole Philippine archipelago. To the expansionists of 1898 here was the miraculous opportunity to keep step in the East with the powers of Europe and with Japan and prevent exclusion from the commerce of Asia. The Philippines would be the Hong Kong, the Kiaochow, the Port Arthur of the United States in the Far East, with a string of island bases and cable stations communicating with them from the Pacific Coast. From the new possession could be pursued the traditional American policy of conserving the independence and territorial integrity of China. It never occurred to these hasty thinkers that trade with a partitioned China might be greater and richer than trade with a preserved China. There was a widespread belief that the American home market for manufactures and native products had become saturated, and their minds played on this. Few could foresee how the tremendous internal development and transformation of the United States within the next generation would multiply the capacity of its people to consume. It seemed then that the markets of the East were the great vents of the future for a competitive industrial society based on capitalistic nationalism. The Philippines would be the American vestibule to the fabulous trade of the Orient. It appears never to have dawned on these adventurers into eastern imperialism that it would be difficult if not impossible to defend those distant islands, there on the other side of the globe, in case the balance of diplomatic power in the Far East should be upset by the complete dominance of any one naval power. They did not glimpse the future collapse of the Occident and the coincident rise of Japan.

Against these champions of a new adventure arose an opposition, dominated by New England intellectuals and organized into the Anti-Imperialist League. They argued on grounds of policy and morality against territorial expansion in the East and the dominion over alien peoples in distant islands in a way never envisaged by the Fathers of the American nation. Their most eloquent spokesman was Senator George F. Hoar, of Worcester, Massachusetts.

In the last analysis it is President McKinley who must bear the responsibility of the acquisition of the Philippines, as well as of the war with Spain, for it is he who commanded the army and navy, and who dictated the instructions to the American plenipotentiaries at Paris. When the peace Commission left the United States its instructions were indecisive as to the Philippines: a pledge to civilization, duty, humanity, a new opening for trade, and general morality, said the President, made it impossible to accept less than the cession in full right and sovereignty of the island of Luzon.

At Paris the Commissioners were perplexed and divided among themselves how much more to take. They held hearings of army officers and other persons (excluding any Filipinos), who had special knowledge of the Philippines and the East. General Merritt, who had commanded the first expeditionary force, pointed out that it would be easier to hold all the islands than one. It was apparent that other powers would step in where the United States left a foothold. Obviously from the strategical point of view, which was an important one, it was a question of taking the whole archipelago or nothing. Senator Gray, the Democratic member of the peace Commission and a steadfast opponent of imperialism, was opposed to taking anything. Judge Day, recently Secretary of State, favored retention of three islands: Luzon, Mindoro, and Palawan, which he thought would afford a sufficient naval base. A majority of the Commission, Senator Frye, Senator Davis, and Mr. Whitelaw Reid, opposed divided control of any kind and wanted the whole archipelago. The President was puzzled what to do. He has left an explanation of how the decision came to him, a statement made to a delegation of clergymen who visited him in Washington a year or so afterward.

"I walked the floor of the White House night after night until midnight," he said, "and I am not ashamed to tell you, gentlemen, that I went down on my knees and prayed Almighty God for light and guidance more than one night. And one night late it came to me this way — I don't know how it was, but it came: (1) That we could not give them back to Spain — that would be cowardly and dishonorable; (2) that we could not turn them over to France [*sic*] or Germany — our commercial rivals in the Orient — that would be bad business and discreditable; (3) that we could not leave them to themselves — they were unfit for self-government — and they would soon have anarchy and misrule over there worse than Spain's was; and (4) that there was nothing left for us to do but to take them all, and to educate the Filipinos, and uplift and civilize and Christianize them, and by God's grace do the very best we could by them, as our fellowmen, for whom Christ also died. And then I went to bed, and to sleep, and slept soundly. . . ."

So the President directed the peace Commission to demand the cession of the whole archipelago. Strangely, the Spanish resisted, and, finally, to smooth the matter over, the American plenipotentiaries actually offered a compensation of $20,000,000. Spain had already agreed to sell out her other Pacific islands to Germany; she now quickly accepted the twenty millions and got out of the East with alacrity.

Peace had come, bringing with it a protectorate over Cuba, and the possession of Puerto Rico, Guam, and the Philippines, in addition to the Hawaiian Islands annexed during the war. Over and above the $20,000,000 paid for this liability in Eastern Asia, the Spanish-American War cost 2910 lives, $250,000,000 war costs, plus the costs of suppressing a two years' native insurrection against American dominion in the Philippines (1000 lives and $170,000,000). It has cost since then to date $919,369,440.38 in pensions, but that cost is due to domestic folly, not war itself. A balance sheet in 1929 of material profits and losses on the account of the Filipinos with the people of the United States since the occupation of the islands, showed only losses for the Americans, profits for the Filipinos. There was also the long accumulation of ill-will against American sovereignty, despite its good works.

The Senate of the United States ratified the treaty by the narrow margin of two votes: 57–27 (February 6, 1899). After the final vote on ratification, it rejected a resolution promising ultimate independence to the Philippines. This resolution met defeat by the casting vote of the Vice President, who thus won himself a remembered place in history: Garret A. Hobart is the name. Meanwhile Aguinaldo and his heroic followers had determined to fight it out to the end against the American occupants. President McKinley and his party leaders, and the Republican newspapers, had appealed successfully in the Congressional elections of 1898 to return Republicans to Congress so that the task of the peace Commissioners in dealing with Spain would be the easier. In the Senate, Senator Lodge, leader of the imperialists, said that to reject the treaty would be to repudiate the President and humiliate the country in the eyes of the civilized world. The President in fact had proclaimed sovereignty over the islands already (December 21, 1898) before the Senate voted on the treaty. Nevertheless there was enough opposition to defeat the treaty until William Jennings Bryan, anti-imperialist and titular leader of the Democratic Party, went to Washington and advised senators of his party to vote for the treaty in order to end the war. He wanted to subordinate the issue of imperialism to that of free-silver in the next presidential election. For imagined political advantages the Democrats sacrificed their principle. The issue of imperialism, like that of the League of Nations twenty years later, showed how foreign affairs are frequently made the football of party politics in the United States. . . .

The American people entered into the war with Spain without counting in advance the costs in men and treasure, and they made peace with little heed to the commitments it involved or the possibility of further wars and expenditures much greater in size, which those commitments might bring in another generation. The chief advantages of the victory were the control of the Caribbean and of the ocean approaches to the future isthmian canal; but it is doubtful whether an aggressive billion-and-a-half-dollar war was necessary to obtain these. Today few citizens

of the United States would wish to undo the results of the Spanish-American War so far as the Caribbean is concerned, but most of them fervently regret the results of that war in the Far East. Not so did men think in 1900. In that year McKinley and his party were re-elected. Looking back on those years of adolescent irresponsibility we can now see the acquisition of the Philippines, the climax of American expansion, as a great national aberration.

The Philippine Islands under the sovereignty of the United States became a monument to American good works and good will, a model for colonial dominion and administration in the world. They also became a military and a diplomatic liability. They were the Achilles' heel of American defense, a hostage to Japan for American foreign policy in the Far East. In the chapters that follow we shall see how time and again Theodore Roosevelt and other American diplomatists had to make concessions to Japanese aggression on the Continent of Asia in return for Japanese disavowal, either explicit or implicit, of aggressive intentions toward the Philippines. The principal concern of the United States in the Islands became that of liquidating decently and honorably an uncomfortable imperialism there, leaving them able to sustain their independence in a sea of sharks. In the Second World War they served as a battle ground for a magnificent rear-guard action that may have held up the Japanese juggernaut just long enough to make all the difference between final defeat or victory for the United Nations in that conflict. But it wasn't planned that way in 1898.

Tyler Dennett: THE PHILIPPINES

IN 1898, at the end of one hundred and fourteen years of relations with the Pacific and Asia, the political aspects of the Far Eastern question were for the first time presented for the serious consideration of the American people in definite proposals for the annexation of the Hawaiian Islands and the cession of the Philippines.

There had been brief, fragmentary and partisan discussions in Congress in 1843 when the Cushing Mission was authorized, in 1852 when the Perry Expedition was on its way eastward, and for the remainder of the sixth decade of the century Congress had kept a sharp eye on the condition of affairs as is indicated by the publication during that period of the entire diplomatic correspondence with China — more than twenty-five hundred pages of documents. Indeed the first years of the Buchanan administration occupied, in relation to Far Eastern affairs, a somewhat similar position to the first years of the McKinley administration. In each case the nation, having recovered from a period of financial depression and panic, found itself with a surplus of produce for which a foreign market seemed desirable and necessary. In both instances the new mercantile energy of the American people was contemporaneous with disorganization and uncertainty in the Far East to which was joined the fear that other nations might seize the opportunity to obtain preferred positions and perhaps to close the doors. In both cases Great Britain found in the United States a sufficient encouragement to justify approaches to the American Government with a view to the achievement of a cordial understanding if not an alliance for the settlement of the Far Eastern question. Both Buchanan and Hay, who became Secretary of State in September, 1898, were promoted to positions of great influence in American foreign policy from periods of acceptable diplomatic service at the Court of St. James following crises in Anglo-American relations which had brought the American people to the brink of war with England. But in 1857 President Buchanan had been so sure of the general indifference of the American people that he had not even presented the Far Eastern question to them for consideration, whereas forty years later McKinley had neither the disposition nor the power to keep it from them.

The same identical questions which had been decided by Marcy, Buchanan and Cass in the later fifties, reappeared in the late nineties. Indeed these questions, though often decided, had never been disposed of. Seward had faced them; so had Fish, Frelinghuysen, Blaine, Bayard and Gresham. They were: Should the United States establish protectorates or acquire territory in the Pacific and the Far East? To what extent should the United States take action to assert and to maintain the open door in China and to sustain its sovereignty and integrity? What were the limits to the degree of cooperation which should be established between the United States and Great Britain in the pursuit of a common object and policy? The broad outlines of the

From Tyler Dennett, *Americans in Eastern Asia; A Critical Study of the Policy of the United States with References to China, Japan and Korea in the 19th Century* (New York: The Macmillan Company, 1922), pp. 607–609, 615–632. Used by permission.

American problem in Asia had not changed in forty years; no, not in more than half a century. The task of Caleb Cushing in 1844 had been to obtain for Americans a non-territorial equivalent for Hongkong. He had only partially succeeded. The task for American statesmen in the last three years of the century was to obtain for Americans a real equivalent, territorial or otherwise, not merely for Hongkong but now also for Kwangchow-wan, Foochow, Tsingtao, Wei-hai-wei and Port Arthur, spheres of influence, and the non-alienation agreements of five powers. The reason why the task had gone so long unfinished was merely that the American people had not cared enough about the markets of Asia to finish it. But in March, 1897, the month of McKinley's inauguration, American steel rails began to sell in the European markets at $18 a ton, and this was assumed to indicate that at length the American people had reached the point in their industrial development where they could no longer safely neglect the markets of the world. It was believed by McKinley, by Mark Hanna, perhaps by John Hay, and by some, though not all capitalists and "captains of industry," that the American people were now ready to resume the task for which the policy of Daniel Webster and Caleb Cushing had proved to be so inadequate. . . .

No relation whatever can be established between the outbreak of hostilities with Spain and the Far Eastern question except that there was a concurrence of dates in the disturbed conditions in China and the climax of the often recurring disturbances in Cuba, and that both synchronized with the expansive movement in American trade which had followed the recovery from the Panic of 1893. The Sino-Japanese War had caused a very notable strengthening of Continental fleets in Chinese waters.

Notwithstanding the warnings of naval officers frequently offered in the last quarter of a century, the Americans were without a naval base in the Far East. Therefore at the outbreak of the Spanish-American War the American fleet in the Far East was left by the declarations of neutrality of Japan, China and Great Britain, in a position which required either a retirement of the fleet to Honolulu from which a declaration of neutrality by the Hawaiian Republic might have barred it, or an attack upon Manila. The retirement of the American forces from the Far East in the spring of 1898 when the Chinese Empire was in such precarious condition would have resulted in a very great loss of American prestige and perhaps an attack upon American life and property, for the Chinese had always been quick to interpret such events as an involuntary weakening of a foreign power. American shipping, also, would have been exposed to attack from the Spanish fleet at Manila.

The attack upon Manila by the American forces was not, however, accidental or unforeseen. Commodore George Dewey was ordered to Japan (October 21, 1897) to assume command of the Far Eastern Squadron. Ten days after the destruction of the U.S.S. *Maine* at Havana Harbor Dewey was instructed to hold himself in readiness to engage the Spanish Squadron at Manila and to conduct offensive operations against the Philippines. The intent of these orders, however, appears plainly to have been to remove the menace of the Spanish fleet rather than to acquire Manila.

The American fleet was ordered to rendezvous at Hongkong and measures were immediately taken to secure adequate supplies. Dewey was even prepared to ignore any declaration of neutrality which might be made by the Chinese Empire. He was informed that Japan, which at that time was badly frightened by the presence of such large European forces in the East, would maintain the most scrupulous neutrality – a neutrality which, nevertheless, Japan was induced to relax slightly a few months after the war broke out. Upon the announcement that a state of hostilities existed between the United States and Spain (there was no declaration of war by either side) the British representatives at Hongkong requested the American fleet to leave by 4 P.M., April 25. Commodore Dewey complied and with no unnecessary delay proceeded to Manila Bay. The battle of May 1st with its swift and brilliant victory left Dewey in control of the bay, with the city in his power. Owing to the lack of sufficient landing force Dewey refrained from occupying the city which he would have been unable to police. Manila was not taken until August 13 and then after some little resistance which probably would not have been presented had the Americans been prepared on May 1st to reap the fruits of their naval victory.

Two concurrent events, significant in a study of policy, demand attention.

There had been incipient or open rebellion in the Philippines for more than a decade. The execution by the Spanish authorities of Dr. José Rizal, the Filipino patriot, December 30, 1896, had produced a short-lived insurrection which was suspended early in 1897 by the arrival of Spanish reinforcements and the agreement of the rebel leaders, Andres Bonifacio and Emilio Aguinaldo, upon the payment of several hundred thousand dollars, to retire from the island. These men went to Hongkong and established a Filipino Junta with the money thus

obtained and were able to continue their patriotic agitation. This Junta formally sought the intervention and protection of the United States and later proposed an alliance. The insurgents had previously sought the aid of Japan. Early in 1898 there were insurrections in both Luzon and Cebu. In April, 1898, Commodore Dewey had several conferences with the Filipino leaders at Hongkong, and in the latter part of the month E. Spencer Pratt, United States consul general at Singapore, had an interview with Aguinaldo, recently arrived from Hongkong, and appears to have proposed to him that he return to China, join Dewey's forces, and accompany the Americans to Manila with a view to assisting them in the Philippines just as Gomez and Garcia had been helping the American forces in Cuba, by promoting insurrection against the Spanish authority. Dewey approved of the suggestion and May 19 Aguinaldo was brought to Manila in the U. S. dispatch boat *McColloch,* upon Dewey's order. While Dewey was careful to make no promises to Aguinaldo, he did give no little encouragement and turned over to him the arsenal at Cavite and permitted him to organize his insurgent forces within the American lines. Consul General Rounseville Wildman had also assisted the insurrectos to purchase arms in Hongkong. Aguinaldo gave out the statement to the Filipinos that the United States would assist the insurrectos.

It does not appear that Admiral Dewey or any of the American representatives in contact with the insurgents before the arrival of the first expeditionary forces June 30, had any suspicion that the United States would acquire the Philippines. "Every American citizen who came in contact with the Filipinos at the inception of the Spanish War," stated General

Thomas M. Anderson, who was the first to give to Dewey the news that there was talk in the United States of the retention of the Islands, "or at any time within a few months after hostilities began probably told those he talked with . . . that we intended to free them from Spanish oppression." In other words, Consul General Pratt, Admiral Dewey, and many more were reaffirming what had been stated hundreds of times by American representatives in the East since the days in 1832 when Edmund Roberts made his treaties, viz., that the United States had neither the intention nor the constitutional right to acquire colonies. In support of this opinion there was also the very recent declaration of President McKinley at the outbreak of the war that the acquisition of territory was not the purpose of the United States.

The Filipino insurgents appear, however, to have considered the possibility that the American Government might alter its traditional policy, and to have decided that at any rate it would be well to accept such aid as was being immediately offered and to meet future problems as they arose. Aguinaldo organized a government on June 12, proclaimed a provisional constitution June 23, and on August 6, a week before the American forces occupied Manila, issued an appeal to the nations of the world for recognition of the independence and belligerency of his government. Meanwhile the insurrectos established military control over part of Luzon.

The second significant event of this period was the action of the three European powers which only three years before had intervened to demand the recession of the Liaotung peninsula to China and subsequently forced the Empire to lease the various ports already referred to as well as to grant the spheres of influ-

ence. Germany, especially, had revealed an alarming land-hunger, and was known to be intriguing in Europe to bring about intervention in the Spanish-American war. At Hongkong Prince Henry, the Kaiser's brother, who had been dispatched to China to make sure of the lease of Kiaochow, remarked to Dewey that he did not believe that the European powers would permit the United States to retain Cuba. Shortly after May first two German cruisers appeared at Manila and other German war vessels followed. Indeed a transport with 1200 reserves was anchored in the harbor for a month. Vice Admiral von Dietrichs stated to Dewey rather sharply: "I am here by order of the Kaiser, sir," and proceeded to show a notable indifference to the blockade regulations which Dewey had established. The German force at the end of June was larger than the blockading squadron. At the same time the Germans sustained very intimate relations with the Spanish authorities within the uncaptured city, and made themselves familiar with the military situation. President McKinley is reported to have believed that war with Germany was imminent.

Meanwhile the ranking officer of the British naval vessels, Admiral Chichester, also observing the proceedings, upon orders from his government fully sustained Dewey's blockade regulations, and on August thirteenth when the American fleet proceeded to attack the city in cooperation with the American land forces, the British Admiral moved H.M.S. *Immortalité* to a point which placed it between the American fleet and the vessels of the European powers. Upon receiving notice that the city had surrendered to the Americans, the British vessel alone offered a salute to the American flag.

The peace negotiations between the United States and Spain began July 22, with a message from the Queen to President McKinley, transmitted through Jules Cambon, the French Ambassador at Washington. To the inquiry of the Queen as to the possible terms of peace the President replied, July 30, stipulating (1) the relinquishment by Spain of Cuba; (2) the cession of to the United States, and the evacuation by Spain of the islands of Porto Rico and the other islands now under sovereignty of Spain in the West Indies, and also the cession of an island in the Ladrones to be selected by the United States; (3) the right to occupy and hold "the city, bay and harbor of Manila pending the conclusion of a treaty of peace which shall determine the control, disposition, and the government of the Philippines." The question of pecuniary indemnity was reserved for subsequent discussion. The stipulation for the cession of an island in the Ladrones had reference to a cable station which, as already noted, had become necessary because of the monopoly of the Great Northern Telegraph Company in Japan and China. The carefully drawn specifications as to Manila and the Philippines indicates either that McKinley, encouraged by the decision of Congress on the Hawaiian annexation, had already determined to hold some part of the Philippines if possible, or at least that he was giving this question close consideration. It must have been quite obvious to any one familiar with the dispatches from Tokio, Seoul and Peking in the summer of 1898, that the Philippines offered a most important strategic position for the United States in case the threatened partition of China along the lines of the spheres of influence should take place. A close study of the trade conditions during the century since the American flag first appeared in Manila Bay, would have indicated that the commercial value of the Islands was of very much less importance than the strategic advantages.

"The terms relating to the Philippines seem," replied the Spanish Minister of State (August 7) "to our understanding, to be quite indefinite." He pointed out that the Spanish flag still waved over Manila and that the control of Spain of the archipelago was still unquestioned by any military operations. However, the protocol, signed August 12, contained the stipulation with reference to the Philippines substantially as outlined by President McKinley twelve days before.

In his instructions to the Peace Commissioners (September 16) the President revealed an expanding purpose in the Far East by ordering them to demand "the cession in full right and sovereignty of the island of Luzon, and equal port and trade rights with the Spanish in all unceded territory in the islands." McKinley elaborated his reasons for these demands:

Without any original thought of complete or even partial acquisition, the presence and success of our arms at Manila imposes upon us obligations which we cannot disregard. The march of events rules and overrules human action. Avowing unreservedly the purpose which has animated all our efforts, and still solicitous to adhere to it, we can not be unmindful that without any desire or design on our part the war has brought us new duties and responsibilities which we must meet and discharge as becomes a great nation on whose growth and career from the beginning the Ruler of Nations has plainly written the high command and pledge of civilization.

The above paragraph was obviously a reference to the alarming international situation in the Far East. Asia was in imminent danger of a convulsion which, once started, could hardly have failed to involve the entire world. The Philippines were unlikely to remain long in the hands of Spain which, impoverished by war, was unable to defend them and badly in need of money. Either by conquest or by purchase they would very probably fall into the out-stretched hands of some waiting European power — very likely Germany — if the Americans were to stand aside.

"Incidental to our tenure of the Philippines is the commercial opportunity to which American statesmanship can not be indifferent," continued McKinley. "It is just to use every legitimate means for the enlargement of American trade; but we seek no advantages in the Orient which are not common to all. Asking only the open door for ourselves, we are ready to accord the open door to others. The commercial opportunity which is naturally and inevitably associated with this new opening depends less on large territorial possessions than upon an adequate commercial basis and upon broad and equal privileges."

This, the first use in an American document of the "open door" phrase, establishes the connection between McKinley's Chinese and Philippines policies. A fortuitous concurrence of events had brought within American grasp the very expedient which Commodore Perry and Dr. Peter Parker had urged in 1853 and 1857. Manila might become the equivalent for Hongkong, and the leased ports of China, for the lack of which American trade and interests in the Far East were, in the summer of 1898, in serious prospective if not present embarrassment.

Exactly forty days after signing the instructions to the Peace Commissioners who had departed immediately for Paris where the conference was held, Secretary of State Hay (October 26) still further enlarged the American demands by cabling to the Commissioners:

The information which has come to the President since your departure convinces him that the acceptance of the cession of Luzon alone, leaving the rest of the islands subject to Spanish rule, or to be the subject of future contention, can not be justified on political, commercial, or humanitarian grounds. The cession must be of the whole of the archipelago or none. The latter is wholly inadmissible and the former must therefore be required.

The precise nature of the information which induced McKinley thus to increase his demands would appear to have been gathered from the reports of the American military and naval authorities and from the diplomatic correspondence from the various foreign capitals in both the East and the West. While Admiral Dewey had thought so little of the first German interference at Manila that at first he had not even made a report upon it, the facts were reported to Europe or London by at least one foreign consul at Manila and were known by the President. Various American military and naval officers from Manila were dispatched to Paris where they appeared before the Peace Commissioners in October and expressed themselves very frankly. Russia was reported to be desirous of establishing at least a naval base in the islands. It was very unlikely that France, the possessions of which in South China were most immediately concerned, would let such another opportunity pass unutilized. Japan, fearful whether in another scramble for islands she might not be separated from Formosa as she had been from Port Arthur, was very desirous that the Philippines be brought under American protection, though not unwilling to effect an understanding with the United States by which the Empire could share in the possession of the islands. Great Britain was alarmed at the prospect of the increase of European influence so near Hongkong, Singapore and her South Pacific possessions. The arguments against the retention by the United States either of a mere naval base or of the island of Luzon were, from the standpoint of military and political affairs, overwhelming. The complete relinquishment or only partial possession of the islands would have promoted war rather than peace in Asia.

After many protests and with the utmost reluctance Spain, while she "relinquished" all claims to sovereignty over Cuba, "ceded" Porto Rico, Guam and the Philippines to the United States in the Treaty of Paris (December 10, 1898). It was agreed also in lieu of the assumption by the United States of the Spanish debt in Cuba or the Philippines, that Spain should receive $20,000,000 for the Philippines.

Five phases of the debates in Congress over the annexation of Hawaii and the Philippines may be distinguished. It was a partisan contest in which both the Democratic and Republican party leaders kept an eye upon the presidential campaign of 1900. There was the clear-cut legal question as to whether the American Government had the constitutional right to acquire non-contiguous territory not designed to be admitted to statehood in the Union. There was the moral question arising out of the consent-of-the-governed doctrine. There was the economic question which included on its industrial side the fear of the introduction of Asiatic cheap labor and on the commercial side the ambitions of the trade expansionists. There was, also, the question of expediency: All other phases of the subject being dismissed as settled, did political, military or commercial expediency demand annexation? It was one of the greatest debates in American congressional history.

Of the partisan passages in the debate little need be said, although one would like to record them as an illustration of the futile demagogic clap-trap of the politician such as always intrudes itself in popular government. However, neither question was decided on purely partisan lines, and in the final vote on the Treaty of Paris, while several Republicans voted against it, there were enough Democratic and Populist votes to secure the necessary two-thirds approval. At the beginning of 1899 the annexation of the Philippines had become so popular in various parts of the country that the Democratic leaders, Bryan included, deemed it unwise to oppose it. Within six months after Dewey's victory the territorial enlargement of the nation had ceased, in large measure, to be a partisan question.

The constitutional and moral aspects of the choice were discussed in able and elevated manner quite in contrast with the partisan debate. The opinion of Chief Justice Taney in the Dred Scott case was frequently alluded to.[1] Much was made of the fact that both in Hawaii and the Philippines whatever government might be set up after annexation had been accomplished would be without the consent of the governed, and that the transfer of the territories themselves was being advocated without any clear indication of the consent of the people. This argument, strong in fact, lost much of its force from those who while advancing it still maintained that naval bases both at Pearl Harbor and in the Philippines ought to be acquired.

The minority report on the joint resolution for the annexation of Hawaii was presented in the House by Hugh A. Dinsmore who had for two years (1887–9)

[1] "There is certainly no power given by the constitution to the Federal Government to establish or maintain colonies bordering on the United States or at a distance, to be ruled and governed at its own pleasure, nor to enlarge its territorial limits in any way except by the admission of new States."

been the United States Minister Resident at Seoul. Dinsmore argued that the annexation would be neither constitutional nor desirable. "If we acquire Hawaii, it is but the first step in the progress of colonial aggrandizement," stated Dinsmore. "What must we expect if we enter upon a colonial policy? Suppose we set our feet upon territory in the Orient. From that moment we become involved in every European controversy with reference to aggressions and the acquirement of territory there. No longer will our ancient peace abide with us." Much of the opposition to annexation was based on the assumption that by the continuance of a policy of territorial and political isolation it would be possible for the United States to avoid war. Senator George Frisbie Hoar (Massachusetts), although he had already set his face like flint against the acquisition of the Philippines, nevertheless saw the futility of this argument when applied to Hawaii. After a conference with President McKinley in which the latter had told him of the landing of the Japanese immigrants at Honolulu, of the evidence of their military training, of the patent determination of Japan to acquire the islands, Hoar went into the Senate and made a powerful speech in advocacy of annexation. He based his argument largely upon the conviction that the failure to annex at that time would lead to inevitable conflict with Japan at some future date. He pointed out that were a line to be drawn from the point of American territory in the Aleutian Islands nearest Asia to the southernmost point of American territory on the Pacific Coast, Hawaii would lie eastward of that line. The annexation of Hawaii was to Senator Hoar, indeed to most Americans, primarily a measure of coast defense. While Dewey's victory at Manila served to expedite the consideration of the question,

it was the fear of Japanese aggression which carried the greater weight in the debate and it seems probable that this argument alone would have been sufficient to accomplish the annexation.

In the course of the Hawaiian debate practically all the partisan, constitutional, and moral grounds were traversed and in the consideration of the Philippine question no new principles were brought forward. But the facts were in some respects very different. Whatever may have been the intent of the makers of the Constitution in respect to the acquisition of non-contiguous territory for colonial purposes, it is at least certain that no adequate provision had been made for specific constitutional means to meet the situation which developed at Manila after May 1st, 1898. In the first place the American fleet in Manila Bay was in actual danger. The arrival of reinforcements from Spain, the stiffening of either Spanish or Filipino opposition to Dewey's presence, or the intervention of European powers were all possible eventualities. There were the gravest military reasons for strengthening the American forces, and for the occupation of the city of Manila. Additional naval vessels were sent and by the end of July there had arrived from San Francisco an expeditionary force of nearly 11,000 although Dewey had asked for only 5000. The occupation of Manila, August 13, did not greatly alter the military situation even though an armistice had been established. Talk of European intervention still continued, the Germans extended their interest to other islands of the archipelago, and the attitude of the insurrectos was most uncertain. In all probability conflict with the Filipinos might have been avoided had the American Government possessed the power to issue immediately a statement guaranteeing ultimate autonomy to the Islands under an American or even an international protectorate. But no such power existed.

While these facts were sufficient to account for the new aspects of the case presented to Congress in December, 1898, there was another fact of greater actual potency. President McKinley and his advisers at some date which may be clearly fixed as not earlier than May 1, and not later than the end of that month, became persuaded that the retention of at least Manila would be desirable for either military or commercial reasons, or for both. The President became convinced also that the American people would support such a program. It soon became evident, however, that it would be unsafe to retain Manila without taking the entire archipelago for much the same reasons that it had been accepted as unsafe to retain Pearl Harbor without annexing all of the Hawaiian Islands. The result was that a situation was deliberately, as well as of necessity, created in the Philippines which made the debate on the approval of the Treaty of Paris somewhat different from the debate on Hawaii. When Congress met in December, and when the article of the Treaty of Paris was sent to the Senate early in January, there were already more than 15,000 American soldiers, mostly volunteers, in the Islands, and they were in danger of a Filipino uprising. This new situation abounded in opportunities to appeal to American national pride, and placed both the politician and the statesman who viewed with alarm the prospect of colonial possessions in positions where only the wisest of men ought to be. Nothing in all previous American political experience afforded an adequate precedent or guide.

On December 10, 1898, the day the Treaty of Paris was signed, Senator George G. Vest (Missouri) introduced a joint resolution:

That under the Constitution of the United States no power is given to the Federal Government to acquire territory to be held and governed permanently as colonies.

The colonial system of European nations can not be established under our present Constitution, but all territory acquired by the Government, except such small amount as may be necessary for coaling stations, correction of boundaries, and similar governmental purposes, must be acquired and governed with the purpose of ultimately organizing such territory into States suitable for admission into the Union.

Two days later the debate began but the President did not wait for a decision. On December 21, he instructed the War Department to extend the military government already established at Manila over the entire archipelago as rapidly as possible. McKinley described American rights in the islands as acquired by conquest. This instruction, which was a few days later telegraphed to Manila and published, consolidated the opposition of the insurrectos to the United States, whereas the passage of the Vest resolution would probably have prevented the approaching rebellion.

Senator Augustus O. Bacon (Georgia) introduced on January 11 a resolution which also would have prevented the impending rebellion.

That the United States hereby disclaim any disposition or intention to exercise sovereignty, jurisdiction or control over said islands, and assert their determination, when a stable and independent government shall have been duly erected therein entitled to recognition as such, to transfer to said government, upon terms which shall be reasonable and just, all rights secured under the cession by Spain, and to thereupon leave the government and control of the islands to their people.

The passage of this resolution would have given to the Philippines a status similar to that already accorded to Cuba. February 14th, a vote on the Bacon resolution resulted in a tie, and Vice President Hobart cast the deciding vote against it. The same day a joint resolution, previously introduced by Samuel D. McEnery (Louisiana), was passed, 26 to 22, in which it was stated that "it is the intention of the United States to establish on said islands a government suitable to the wants and conditions of the inhabitants of said islands, to prepare for them *local self-government*, and in due time to make such disposition of said islands as will promote the interests of the citizens of the United States and the inhabitants of said islands." Permanent annexation was expressly disavowed. After so much encouragement from the opposition which was conducting an active campaign for immediate withdrawal of the American forces, the Filipinos were less than ever prepared to accept a status as a theoretically conquered people. In point of fact the American forces had not even conquered the island of Luzon. The most that can be said in extenuation is that the policy and the resolution had been adopted in great ignorance of the actual facts in the Islands, and in a blissful and exalted assumption that any race ought to regard conquest by the American people as a superlative blessing.

The vote on the Treaty of Paris was set for February 6. Two days before the vote the insurgents and the American military forces came into actual conflict, and some American soldiers were killed. That this fact influenced the decision of the Senate there can be little doubt. The vote was 57 to 27, three Republican senators voting with the opposition. A change of two votes would have defeated the treaty.

While there would appear to be no foundation for the charge that the American military forces in the Philippines had deliberately brought on the conflict of February 4 with a view of influencing the Senate, it is quite evident that while the treaty was under consideration, the Administration had created a condition in the Islands which in the end exercised a coercing influence on the Senate. That such a policy had appeared to be necessary at the time reveals how utterly inadequate are the provisions of the American Constitution enabling the government to initiate wise preventive measures to meet such threatening situations as were now constantly recurring in Asia.

"The war that followed it," wrote Senator Hoar seven years later, "crushed the Republic that the Philippine people had set up for themselves, deprived them of their independence, and established there, by American power, a government in which the people have no part, against their will. No man, I think, will seriously question that that action was contrary to the Declaration of Independence, the fundamental principles declared in many State constitutions, the principles avowed by the founders of the Republic, and by our statesmen of all parties down to a time long after the death of Lincoln."

Such a passage, which was and is still more or less characteristic of the opposition to the acquisition of the Islands, is worthy of note. It assumed what was not true. The Filipinos had not set up a "republic"; the nature of the government which they would select, or which Aguinaldo and his advisers would have selected for them, was not clear, and the measures which they had actually adopted by February 1, 1899, by no means prove that they were likely to set up democratic institutions. The rebellion arose not in support of a republic but in opposition to the proposed conquest by the United States.

But even were one to grant the entire truth of every similar assertion made by Senator Hoar and so many others, one need not reach his conclusion in the absence of any constructive suggestion for dealing with the international situation as it existed in the Far East in 1898. Nowhere in the debates on the Philippine question does one find any adequate meeting of the facts by the opponents of the Administration policy. Granted that the President, his advisers and the military diplomats at Manila blundered into very unnecessary and tactless positions before the Filipinos, yet what else was there to do but to remain and to extend the American domain to the entire archipelago? To have retired would, at the worst, have precipitated war in the Far East, or, at the best, it would have created another Korea.

The more important conclusions to which we may come from a study of these events are: (1) The United States could not withdraw from the Philippines in 1898. (2) Notwithstanding the opposition of a very considerable section of the American people, the majority, led by the Administration, clearly wished the Philippines to be retained. (3) The diplomatic negotiations with the Filipinos were badly handled and the President, while declining to exceed his constitutional powers by granting the "tangible concessions" desired, did none the less severely strain his executive war-making authority by ordering the extension of the military

government over the archipelago, which was equivalent to authorizing a campaign of conquest, while the Senate was discussing the question. (4) McKinley created a situation in the Philippines either because of supposed military necessity or because of the international situation, which had the effect of coercing the Senate. (5) Like Cass's instructions to Reed in 1857, and like Seward's policy in Japan and his proposed policy in Korea, the McKinley policy in 1898 was profoundly influenced by the desire to assert American rights in the East in the face of European aggression.

The McKinley policy in the Philippines was not new: it was a return in principle to the policy of Seward. Fundamentally it was not a departure from but a continuance of traditional American policy in Asia, for it was exerted in the interest of the open door and of sustaining China, yes, of sustaining Asia against the aggressions of Europe. It was, however, a reversal of American policy as it had been applied so futilely in Korea since 1882. Notwithstanding the Filipino insurrection, the anti-foreign outbreak in China, and the annoyance of many Japanese at the increase of American domain, the United States was at the end of the century more nearly allied, by political and commercial necessity, to Asia, and to Asiatic aspirations, than to Europe.

The most unfortunate feature of the entire debate had been that it was settled without any clear understanding by the American people of the relation of Hawaii and the Philippines to the still larger question of American policy in Asia.

Suggestions for Additional Reading

The most complete single study of American imperialism in 1898 is Julius W. Pratt, *Expansionists of 1898* (Baltimore, 1936). Less scholarly but delightful reading and valuable for its insights into the popular temper of the time is Walter Millis, *The Martial Spirit* (Boston, 1931). A brilliant and biting analysis of the ideology of expansionism throughout our history is provided in Albert Weinberg, *Manifest Destiny* (Baltimore, 1935). For a sophisticated treatment placing the small group of influential imperialist leaders in their social and political context, see the early pages of Matthew Josephson, *The President Makers, 1896–1912* (New York, 1940). Further knowledge on two crucial personalities in these years is afforded by two biographies: Henry F. Pringle, *Theodore Roosevelt* (New York, 1931) and Charles S. Olcott, *The Life of William McKinley* (Boston, 1916). Chapters XXX and XXXI of Thomas A. Bailey's *Diplomatic History of the American People* (New York, 1950) give a concise account of the war and the debate over the Philippines with particular attention to the internal pressures for both decisions.

Many books are available for placing American imperialism in its world context. See, for example: William L. Langer, *The Diplomacy of Imperialism* (New York, 1951); Parker T. Moon, *Imperialism and World Politics* (New York, 1926); Paul S. Reinsch, *World Politics* (New York, 1900).

The relation between imperialism and capitalism has been and continues to be a subject of controversy. The reader may well wish to supplement the brief selection from Hobson's book with more extended reading in the original, John A. Hobson, *Imperialism, A Study* (London, 1938). For a similar analysis written by an American shortly before 1898, an article which may have served as the inspiration for many of Hobson's ideas, see "The Economic Basis of Imperialism" in Charles A. Conant, *The United States in the Orient* (Boston, 1901). Neo-Marxist views of imperialism are vigorously stated in Nikolai Lenin, *Imperialism, The Last Stage in the Development of Capitalism* (Detroit, 1924) and in Paul M. Sweezy, *The Theory of Capitalist Development* (New York, 1942). An American economist, Earl M. Winslow, in *The Pattern of Imperialism* (New York, 1948) marshals counter arguments in support of the view that capitalism is naturally and essentially hostile to imperialism. Winslow has also written a brief review of various viewpoints in "Marxian, Liberal, and Sociological Theories of Imperialism," *Journal of Political Economy*, 39 (1931), 713–758.

Further evidence on the forces which aroused the public clamor for war is available in Marcus M. Wilkerson, *Public Opinion and the Spanish-American War* (Baton Rouge, 1932) and in two articles by G. W. Auxier: "Middle Western Newspapers and the Spanish-American War, 1895–1898," *Mississippi Valley Historical Review*, 26 (1940), 523–534 and "The Propaganda Activities of the Cuban *Junta* in Precipitating the Spanish-American War, 1895–1898," *Hispanic American Historical Review*, 19 (1939), 286–305. In the first of these articles Auxier contends that Middle Western papers were less influenced by the sensational journals of New York than Wisan indicated but that the papers of this area had their own more rational arguments for war.

Political considerations influencing the Senate's vote on the treaty which ended the war and secured the Philippines are examined closely by W. Stull Holt in *Treaties Defeated by the Senate* (Baltimore, 1933). The opposition to imperialism has been described in F. H. Harrington, "The Anti-Imperialist Movement in the United States, 1898–1900," *Mississippi Valley Historical Review*, 22 (1935), 211–230 and in the same author's "Literary Aspects of American Anti-Imperialism, 1898–1902," *New England Quarterly*, 10 (1937), 650–667. The controversy over imperialism stirred many contemporary writers to eloquent statements of their views about America's particular mission in the world. Rudyard Kipling's influential poetic plea for American expansion, "The White Man's Burden," was first published in the February, 1899, issue of *McClure's* Magazine. It can be found reprinted in many anthologies. Examples of the best anti-imperialist writings are the following: William Graham Sumner, *The Conquest of the United States by Spain* (Boston, 1899); William Vaughn Moody, "An Ode in Time of Hesitation," *Poems* (Boston, 1901), also included in many anthologies; and Mark Twain, "To the Person Sitting in Darkness," *North American Review*, 172 (1901), 161–176. The "Mr. Dooley" essay by Finley Peter Dunne on "Expansion" is a brief classic in American humor. It is included in Elmer Ellis's edition of *Mr. Dooley at His Best* (New York, 1938).

Debate as to whether the United States should withdraw from the Philippines continued unabated up to the final grant of independence to the islands at the close of World War II. In 1926 Moorfield Storey and H. P. Lichauco published *The Conquest of the Philippines by the United States, 1898–1925* (New York, 1926), a bitter account of American treatment of the Filipinos. Rufus S. Tucker made an attempt in 1929 to determine whether the Philippines had been financially profitable to the United States: "A Balance Sheet of the Philippines," *Harvard Business Review*, 8 (1829), 10–23. Some years later Grayson L. Kirk re-examined the question of *Philippine Independence* (New York, 1836). Most recently Julius W. Pratt has surveyed the whole story of American empire in *America's Colonial Experiment* (New York, 1950), while G. A. Grunder and W. E. Livezey have published a fine review of American experience with the Philippines in *The Philippines and the United States* (Norman, Okla., 1952).

The ablest treatment of our relations with the Far East as they have developed since 1898 is A. Whitney Griswold, *Far Eastern Policy of the United States* (New York, 1938). A provocative analysis of characteristic American concepts and reactions in the conduct of our foreign policy beginning with the Spanish-American War is the recent collection of lectures by George F. Kennan, *American Diplomacy, 1900–1950* (New York, 1950).